Technology and Social Transformations in Hospitality, Tourism and Gastronomy: South Asia Perspectives

———————————————

Technology and Social Transformations in Hospitality, Tourism and Gastronomy: South Asia Perspectives

Edited by

Savita Sharma

Shri Vishwakarma Skill University, India

Shivam Bhartiya

Central University of Karnataka, India

CABI is a trading name of CAB International

CABI
Nosworthy Way
Wallingford
Oxfordshire OX10 8DE
UK

Tel: +44 (0)1491 832111
E-mail: info@cabi.org
Website: www.cabi.org

CABI
200 Portland Street
Boston
MA 02114
USA

T: +1 (617)682-9015
E-mail: cabi-nao@cabi.org

The views expressed in this publication are those of the author(s) and do not necessarily represent those of, and should not be attributed to, CAB International (CABI). Any images, figures and tables not otherwise attributed are the author(s)' own. References to internet websites (URLs) were accurate at the time of writing.

CAB International and, where different, the copyright owner shall not be liable for technical or other errors or omissions contained herein. The information is supplied without obligation and on the understanding that any person who acts upon it, or otherwise changes their position in reliance thereon, does so entirely at their own risk. Information supplied is neither intended nor implied to be a substitute for professional advice. The reader/user accepts all risks and responsibility for losses, damages, costs and other consequences resulting directly or indirectly from using this information.

CABI's Terms and Conditions, including its full disclaimer, may be found at https://www.cabi.org/terms-and-conditions/.

A catalogue record for this book is available from the British Library, London, UK.

ISBN-13: 9781800621220 (hardback)
         9781800621237 (ePDF)
         9781800621244 (ePub)

DOI: 10.1079/9781800621244.0000

Commissioning Editor: Claire Parfitt
Editorial Assistant: Emma McCann
Production Editor: Marta Patiño

Typeset by Exeter Premedia Services Pvt Ltd, Chennai, India
Printed and bound in the USA by Integrated Books International, Dulles, Virginia

Contents

Contributors

Abdullah, Omar, Amity School of Hospitality, Amity University, Noida, Uttar Pradesh, India; email: omarwani93@gmail.com

Attri, Kamlesh, Department of Commerce, Shyam Lal College, University of Delhi, New Delhi, India; email: kamlesh_atri81@yahoo.co.in

Bhartiya, Shivam, Department of Tourism & Hotel Management, Central University of Karnataka, Kalaburagi, Karnataka, India; email: shivam.prakash84@gmail.com

Bhatt, Vaibhav, Department of Tourism and Hospitality Management, Central University of Tamil Nadu, Tamil Nadu, India; email: vaibhavbhatt@cutn.ac.in

Chhetri, Sonali, Department of Hospitality Management, CT University, Ludhiana, Punjab, India; email: sonalitiwari0302@gmail.com

Dhodi, R.K., Centre for Mountain Tourism and Hospitality Studies, HNB Garhwal Central University, Srinagar (G), Uttarakhand, India; email: dhodirakesh@gmail.com

Dhodi, Rashmi, Centre for Mountain Tourism and Hospitality Studies, HNB Garhwal Central University, Srinagar (G), Uttarakhand, India; email: rashmi.cmths@gmail.com

Hassan, Afsheen, Superior University, Lahore, Pakistan; email: afsheen.hassan@superior.edu.pk

Khurana, Amandeep, Institute of Hotel Management, Gurdaspur, Punjab, India; email: mnkhurana325@gmail.com

Kumar, Amit, School of Hotel Management, Airlines and Tourism, CT University, Ludhiana, Punjab, India; email: amit.17044@ctuniversity.in

Kumar, Sanjeev, Institute of Hotel and Tourism Management, Maharishi Dayananda University, Rohtak, Haryana, India; email: sanjeev.rawal30@gmail.com

Kumar, Suneel, Department of Commerce, Shaheed Bhagat Singh College, University of Delhi, New Delhi, India; email: drsuneel.sbsc@gmail.com

Kumar, Varinder, Faculty of Management Studies, University of Delhi, New Delhi, India; email: varinder.phd20@fms.edu

Maitra, Rekha, Department of Travel and Tourism Management, DAV Centenary College, Faridabad, Haryana, India; email: rekhavmaitra@gmail.com

Nadalipour, Zahra, University of Science and Culture, Tehran, Iran; email: z.nadalipour@usc.ac.ir

Pareek, Teena, School of Management, JECRC University, Jaipur, Rajasthan, India; email: teena.pareek@jecrc.edu.in

Roy, Bindu, Department of Commerce, DAV Centenary College, Faridabad, Haryana, India; email: bindu.roy23@gmail.com

Sahdev, Dilraj Singh, Institute of Hotel Management, Gurdaspur, Punjab, India; email: dilraj78@gmail.com

Shah Hosseini, Fatemeh, University of Science and Culture, Tehran, Iran; email: hossinif329@gmail.com

Sharma, Savita, Skill Faculty of Management Studies & Research, Shri Vishwakarma Skill University, Gurugram, Haryana, India; email: drsharmasavi@gmail.com

Srivastava, Sidharth, School of Management, JECRC University, Jaipur, Rajasthan, India; email: sidharthsrivastava2011@yahoo.in

Sufi, Tahir, Amity School of Hospitality, Amity University, Noida, Uttar Pradesh, India; email: tsufi@amity.edu

Verma, Kuldeep, Centre for Mountain Tourism and Hospitality Studies, HNB Garhwal Central University, Srinagar (G), Uttarakhand, India; email: kuldeepvermabhu@gmail.com

Introduction

———————————

Tourism and gastronomy have been seen as a major force in social and technological transformation in both the developed and developing world. Tourism services offered by nations generate inbound visitors who will spend money in a host destination, which is considered an important way to achieve integrated social, economic and technological development. Therefore, tourism is often cited as being a key factor in the development of the destination globally and to achieve maximum benefit from the industry is vital. The United Nations World Tourism Organization (UNWTO) and several other national and international tourism organizations always consider tourism as a major force in sociocultural, economic and technological development in both the developing and developed nations.

To achieve the maximum benefits from tourism and gastronomy, a range of supporting facilities and services are required. Some of these will be provided by the public sector, but others require cooperation from the private sector in investment and innovation. The tourism and hospitality industry noted high competition in the last few years, and to reduce the risk of losing the market, customers' gastronomy is becoming an increasingly important new tourism product to attract and amuse tourists. It is not only because food is central to the tourist experience, but also because it has become an important identity formation source in modern society.

Contemporary social and technological global conditions have promoted the emergence of new ways of experiencing tourism and gastronomy. These are now not only acting as a driver for economic growth but are also providing opportunities to maximize the multiplier effect. Indeed, there is a growing interest in the social and technological analysis of tourism and gastronomy. Currently several scholarly works on tourism and gastronomy have focused on its role as a driver for social and technological development apart from its economic and marketing significance. The purpose of this book is to present the social and technological transformation process in the destination through tourism and gastronomy. Another aim is to highlight the importance of tourism and gastronomy experiences, not only for tourists but also for the host communities.

The Structure of the Book

In order to explore the approaches of tourism and gastronomy in the transformation process of society and technology, the book considers studies that revolve around tourism, hospitality, gastronomy, social transformation, and technology transformation, and discusses the key factors affecting both developing and developed nations. It comprises nine edited chapters, informed by academics active in these fields of research, and is divided into two sections: the first looks at technological transformation perspectives; the second examines social transformation perspectives. A brief outline of each chapter follows.

Section A: Technological Transformation

Chapter 1: A study on acceptance and implementation of contactless technology in hotels of Amritsar Punjab

Prior to the global pandemic, hotels were far behind the global commerce ecosystem when it came to technology adaptation. Now hoteliers are adopting digital methods, and with the increased adoption of these methods they can now provide guests with an overall better experience, staying competitive and providing digital-savvy travellers with a full digital offering. The hotel industry of the Punjab region is now implementing fewer contact points in order to reconfigure the use of public spaces as well as increasing the number of new pandemic protocols. These newly introduced technologies are providing guests with unforgettable digital experiences during their trip and stay at their destination. Hotels in the Punjab region are now offering keyless check-in and personalizing the guest journey to achieve maximum guest satisfaction scores.

Chapter 2: Increasing tourism resilience with digital engagement in the hotel industry

The tourism and hospitality industries have been hit hard because of the global COVID-19 pandemic. Travel restrictions imposed by governments to keep their populations safe and to control the spread of the disease have meant tremendous upheaval and closures. However, the industry has made positive changes by trying out new ideas to keep business alive and finding creative solutions that they might not have found otherwise. Customers have also shifted their priorities, such as greater emphasis on hygiene and safety. This encouraged the hotel industry to shift how it provides services to customers and to think about what it wants to emphasize when creating an experience for customers. Hence, digital engagement has become an increasingly important part of business success. The hotel industry is tending to adopt new technological ideas to survive the downturn, and to 'think outside the box' in finding solutions that might be far from their normal operation.

Chapter 3: The role of influencers in destination marketing through Instagram social platform

For destination marketing, Instagram has the power to create dynamic experiences that engage travellers by telling the visual story of a destination using photos and videos. Instagram, nowadays, is proving to be an effective social platform for targeting new customers and creating brand awareness. It lets the user know everything a destination has to offer through visuals. Instagram also helps in the promotion of the global community concept. Tourism and hospitality organizations are now using Instagram as part of a multi-channel strategy to target new customers and continually keep them engaged and excited using beautiful images and contextual stories about activities and interests. One survey found that 40% of consumers under 30 are prioritizing 'Instagrammability' of potential destinations when making purchase decisions. This is the Instagram effect, and the travel industry is joining forces with social media to get a slice of it.

Chapter 4: Integration of robotic technology and artificial intelligence in the transformation of the tourism industry: a critical viewpoint

In recent years, the use of digital technologies has accelerated the rise of the digital tourism industry. The tourism industry is always considered one of the fastest growing industries. It is heavily influenced by robotic technology and artificial intelligence. These technologies in the tourism industry are adopted to predict travel possibilities, provide personalized travel support and customized travel needs, improve customer service, and make in-trip and post-trip demand management more streamlined. After the COVID-19 global pandemic, hotels, airports and other places began using robotic technology to reduce human-to-human contact and even artificial intelligence-powered concierges to enhance sanitization and personalization. In this chapter, the authors conclude that robotic technology and artificial intelligence in the tourism industry can assist in making travellers' experiences more comfortable and convenient. Digital technologies, like the use of robots, and artificial intelligence-enabled services are playing an increasingly important role in the evolution of the tourism industry, providing a variety of ways to enhance the tourist experience.

Chapter 5: The influence of Instagram on Generation Z travel motivation and destination choice making to the actual travelling

The social media platform Instagram plays a major role in the lives of Generation Z travellers and tourism organizations are embracing it as their main promotional channel. For Generation Z, Instagram is the top source of inspiration when deciding on a vacation destination and past research reveals that their motivation, being visual vacationers and social snappers, is not limited to word-of-mouth and brochures. According to a study conducted by Booking.com, about 70% of Generation Z like to see travel posts, pictures and travel videos on social media, and when it comes to selecting destinations to visit, they head straight to social feeds and reviews posted on a social media platform such as Instagram. Many Instagram users say they are interested in travelling somewhere that will look good in an Instagram post.

Section B: Social Transformation

Chapter 6: Service quality perspective and guest satisfaction in food and beverage outlets of five-star hotels of Delhi-NCR

Guest satisfaction and service quality are considered crucial aspects in food and beverage outlets and also for the development of hotels. Good service quality is expected to result in guest satisfaction and therefore increase customer retention, loyalty and advocacy. This study is purely based on the service quality measures and strategies implemented to make guests happy and retain them to maximize profit. Food and beverage outlets have to adjust to the changing tastes and leanings of clients and provide satisfactory service for them. The authors strongly suggest that SERVQUAL factors have an impact on customer satisfaction. Meanwhile, tangible factors of service quality need to be matched to guests' expectations and need to be maintained.

Chapter 7: Exploring the indicators of international tourists' experience on local food of Delhi

With the rise of the tourism industry, many tourist destinations have become more aggressive in expressing their unique food culture to promote the destination. Food has always been an important part of most travel experiences and of creating a destination's image. Today, food has become such a trend that social media platforms are flooded with images of tourists trying food from various parts of the world. This chapter highlights the relationship of food to destination and the benefits of using food as an enhancer of a destination's attractiveness through systematic reviews. It is wise for destinations to use food as a promotional strategy to achieve customer satisfaction, contribute to the authenticity of the destination, strengthen the local economy, and provide an environmentally friendly infrastructure. Governments from different nations also realize that food can bring a lot of good to the economy, building a destination image, preserving culture, supporting agricultural activities and food production, empowering the community, and generating pride and local identity.

Chapter 8: A comparative study on waste management practices in pre-COVID and during-COVID scenarios: an overview of the hotel industry

Hotels and accommodation establishments are places where there is a high degree of interaction among guests and workers. The pandemic has exposed several lapses and limitations of the hotel industry across countries. Managing waste in hotels is one of the major issues, and failures of the waste management system have escalated with the spread of COVID via secondary transmission. Many hotels were already focused on more sustainable operations and waste management before the pandemic, but now they are prioritizing and updating hygiene standards. Dealing with this situation within the hotel industry, along with an influx of new guests as the industry opens up again, they are using robust and comprehensive waste management systems and responsible recycling.

Chapter 9: Can community-based tourism be a catalyst for social transformation?

Community tourism has strong potential to enhance social change across the world through alleviating poverty, broadening information access, improving infrastructure and facilities, and providing new and diverse employment opportunities. The development and promotion of community tourism needs to be strengthened by increasing community involvement and developing tourism in a more sustainable and competitive way. In this chapter, the authors highlight that positive transformation of the social structure of communities is possible through active participation in the tourism development process. Their analysis focuses on economic, sociocultural and environmental aspects, and acknowledges that community tourism has enhanced livelihoods through these aspects.

Section A: Technological Transformation

1 A Study on Acceptance and Implementation of Contactless Technology in Hotels of Amritsar Punjab

Dilraj Singh Shadev* and Amandeep Khurana
Institute of Hotel Management, Gurdaspur, Punjab, India

Abstract

'Technology is an integral part of modern life. It can be utilized to extend the personal human touch.'

Technology has always come to the rescue whenever hard times have pressed upon mankind. Presently, when the COVID-19 pandemic has crippled many flourishing businesses in the hospitality industry, it is for people who are directly or indirectly related to guest services to include and implement technology in hotels that is able to bring back confidence among potential guests to use various services. Contactless technology is one such facility that is very much needed to increase occupancy in hotels, provided that guests and staff both accept the new technology and start using it without any attitudinal issues. The requirement for less face-to-face contact and systematic social distancing is making contactless technology more acceptable in hotels today. By giving a personalized experience to the guest through contactless service, hoteliers can achieve guest satisfaction along with optimum operational results for employees.

This study aims to use the technology acceptance model in studying the perceived ease of use and perceived usefulness of contactless technology among staff in the hotels of Amritsar. The research work will study the acceptance of contactless technology in relation to the behaviour and attitude of staff concerning the technology and will refer to various issues in operationalizing the technology in hotels. The results of this research work will help hoteliers put contactless technology into use in their hotels after considering the behavioural and attitudinal issues of their staff.

Introduction

The hospitality industry has always been the frontrunner in adopting new technology that has the potential to put hotel guests at ease. The pandemic has pushed the industry into the sphere of low-level or zero business, which makes it even more important to adopt such technology that benefits both the guest and the hotel. 'New normal' is the expression that is heard in every field, with new instructions and guidelines. It involves the acceptance of, and training staff to use, new technology in various organizations. With the reopening of business operations, it is vital to have a workforce that is acquainted with the latest technology to hand. In order to cultivate confidence among travellers and potential hotel guests, it is important to access the expectations of guests with respect to these new normal guidelines, especially in regard to contactless technology.

---

*Corresponding author: dilraj78@gmail.com

© CAB International 2023. *Technology and Social Transformations in Hospitality, Tourism and Gastronomy: South Asia Perspectives* (eds S. Sharma and S. Bhartiya)
DOI: 10.1079/9781800621244.0001

Contactless Technology

Some of the areas that can be upgraded with contactless technology are:

- contactless check-in and check-out with digital support;
- contactless food delivery to the room;
- housekeeping services with absolutely no contact with guests;
- contactless amenities;
- minimizing restaurant areas in hotels;
- cashless and contactless payment; and
- being careful in terms of room allocation regarding social distancing.

Since personal contact is often not possible at the present time, safer, viable, self-service methods must be implemented through the adoption of contactless technology, and these are now expected by the guest. They include check-in and check-out kiosks based on self-service, use of mobile applications for navigational guides, contactless in-room entertainment, food and beverage (F&B) service and housekeeping activities, AI-enabled voice assistants, and even robots handled by the concierge.

Before hotels can implement a contactless service for guests, it is important to first identify the vital contact points during the customer's stay through an accurate guest journey map. This will help hotels to understand typical guest-contact points and identify the areas where suitable technology can be introduced to achieve customer satisfaction, even when there is minimum contact with hotel staff.

Some of the benefits of contactless technology could be:

- delivering a safe, seamless, personalized hotel experience;
- automating the accommodation experience from check-in to check-out; and
- using voice technology to engage with guests.

Review of the Literature

The behavioural intention of the individual is stated in a model outlined by Venkatesh and Davis (2000). The main emphasis is on two viewpoints, which are perceived usefulness and perceived ease of use. These two views are further dependent on external variables such as the attitude of employees, compatibility of the technology, habits of employees and intention to use. It is also very clear that perceived usefulness depends on perceived ease of use, and this impacts the overall use of technology in any organization.

Hassan *et al.* (2019) state that perceived ease of use can be classified as the employee's observation that any new technology will improve his or her skills and have a significant impact on their performance. The technology itself should be well defined in terms of its feasibility in addressing the employee's day-to-day issues at work. From the customer's point of view, technology should be needed, so that when it is implemented it will be accepted by customers as being necessary, and this will ultimately affect the attitude of staff in using the technology (Sondhi, 2017). Perceived usefulness of any technology depends on its acceptance among those who are going to use it. Application of technology that is easy to use helps customers as well as staff to meet their individual requirements during their operations, and will always find acceptance as useful technology. The usefulness of any newly implemented system will help customers and employees achieve optimum use of technology in any situation.

According to Sanad (2014), service quality, with reference to adapted technology, plays a vital role in performance. Sanad states that there is a subjective comparison between the actual service received by the customer and the expected service. Service quality is defined by the actual usefulness of the service received by the consumer in relation to the available resources in terms of technology and trained manpower. When it comes to web-based service, it is found in the study done by Alsmydai that there is a relationship between service quality, perceived usefulness and ultimate customer satisfaction. As per Koontz (2010), to gain commitment to achieving goals, true participation in attaining them is essential. Individuals should be encouraged to set them. The manager, of course, should review and approve them. But it is probable that in the proper environment, people tend to set goals higher than their superiors would set them. Participation of the right kind yields both motivation and knowledge that is valuable for enterprise success. Participation is also a means of recognition; it appeals to the need for affiliation and acceptance.

Technological advances are being introduced to organizations at an ever-increasing pace (Le, 2015). Technology is rapidly changing in many areas, such as robotics, in particular. Technology makes it easy to monitor the number of company employees working at home, and as technological advancements continue, many important questions will be raised concerning issues such as performance monitoring and career planning. According to Amrit (2021), the interaction between employees and guests has to be minimized with the help of contactless technology. The hospitality industry has to change its overall view in terms of providing safe contactless service to its customers. It is expected that hotel authorities will change their staff hiring patterns, standard operating procedures, and sales and marketing policies. The main goal of providing social distancing will guide hotels in the future in laying down their policies in accordance with state and national guidelines for COVID-19, also keeping in mind the guests' expectations of high standards of service and building confidence among potential guests.

As discussed by Sorell (2020), hotels nowadays are increasingly removing the touchpoints between guests and staff. This is only possible when contactless technology is implemented at such touchpoints. It is very much understood by all the players in the hospitality industry that new processes are to be implemented and supported by employees so that hoteliers can provide a safe and sanitized environment for their staff and guests. As stated by Silva (2015), many theoretical models have been used and applied to study the acceptance of new technology among employees and staff. Various factors play a vital role in the acceptance of technology. Various models focus on external individual belief systems when it comes to studying the acceptance of technology, such as intention, habit, compatibility, attitude, perceived usefulness and perceived ease of use. Current research focuses on the acceptance of contactless service provided by technology for the hotel guest and the impact of the various factors that play important roles in influencing the attitude of employees towards technology.

Attitude is a crucial idea within the study of advertising and marketing structures (Alsamydai, 2014). It is a crucial part of statistics research, for the generation of the popularity model that predicts perceived ease of use, mindset, aim and use. Attitude is described as a good or bad assessment of people, gadgets, events, activities, ideas, or pretty much anything in the environment.

The idea of mindset and conduct appears to play a crucial function in predicting and understanding individuals' behaviour. The intention towards using technology is very much related to generation. The use of mobile banking for transactions is in the same category.

Having the right technology inside the hotel not only makes a difference to the overall experience of the guest but also helps staff maintain a smooth stay for the guest without coming into contact with them. Contactless technology that supports these kinds of working environments brings satisfaction to the guest. It also helps check-in, contactless valet services and contact tracing to be easier and stress-free. It helps hotel staff to revaluate their jobs and the way the organization helps to make the guest comfortable. When it comes to contactless technology for guest interaction and services, staff (and guests) need simplicity, ease and distance. Fewer interactions at the front desk means more time to focus on other errands that improve the quality of a stay and the value of the staff's work. This might mean that staff are better able to deal with various special requests made by the guest. It could allow staff to conduct more frequent maintenance checks around the property or do back-office tasks.

As the international travel industry has opened up following the pandemic, the use of contactless technology has grown to achieve the industry's primary goal, which is to provide guests with the utmost care and service. The hotel should offer contactless technology at every point of interaction such as check-in, payment, room service and feedback. The hotel should examine the various touchpoints between staff and guests before the guest checks in to (i) evaluate the acceptance of contactless technology by hotel professionals; and (ii) identify the prominent barriers that exist in the implementation of contactless technology.

Research Methodology

The present study was carried out in the context of hotel employees (Table 1.2) who are now becoming familiar with new types of technology that require little or no contact with the guest. In this research, we have tried to understand how well contactless technology will be accepted. Two dimensions were considered: the individual context and the technological context. The individual context comprises variables like attitude, compatibility and intention. The technological context comprises variables such as perceived ease of use (PEU) and perceived usefulness (PU), as proposed by Davis; and habit. For analysing data averages, percentages and Cronbach's alpha were used.

Data collection

The data for the current study are mainly based on two types of resource:

Secondary sources: Data and information obtained from reviewing the literature, research findings, books and websites related to this study.

Primary sources: On the basis of initial information obtained from literature and research findings and various variables such as habit, compatibility, intention and attitude, a questionnaire (Table 1.1) with 26 statements was developed to evaluate the acceptance of contactless technology in terms of its perceived usefulness and perceived ease of use among hotel staff in various hotels in Amritsar. The questionnaire was in English.

The Likert scale was chosen for the scaling technique, with seven scales: 1. Totally disagree; 2. Disagree; 3. Slightly disagree; 4. Neither agree nor disagree; 5. Slightly agree; 6. Agree; 7. Totally agree.

Table 1.1. Questions asked of respondents.

Perceived usefulness

PU1 The use of contactless technology could help me to serve hotel guests efficiently.

PU2 The use of contactless technology may improve the services to my guests.

PU3 The use of contactless technology is compatible with my work requirements.

PU4 The use of contactless technology is necessary to provide safety to hotel guests.

PU5 Contactless technology can facilitate data analysis for decision making.

PU6 Contactless technology can improve my performance in guest handling.

Perceived ease of use

PEU1 I think that I could easily learn how to use contactless technology.

PEU2 I think it would be easy to perform the tasks necessary for the satisfaction of the guest using contactless technology.

PEU3 I think I will find it easy to acquire the necessary skills to use contactless technology.

PEU4 I believe that the services provided through contactless technology would be helpful and easy to understand by the guest.

PEU5 I think that the contactless technology will be easy to use.

Attitude

ATD1 I think it is a good idea to use contactless technology in hotels.

Continued

Table 1.1. Continued

ATD2 Contactless technology could help me get the most out of my time to follow up and get guest feedback.

ATD3 Hotel managers would welcome the fact that I feel it convenient to use contactless technology.

ATD4 Other hotel professionals would welcome the fact that I use contactless technology.

Compatibility

COMP1 The use of contactless technology may imply major changes in my work.

COMP2 I think that contactless technology is a flexible technology to interact with.

COMP3 In general, contactless technology may be useful to improve hotel and guest relations.

COMP4 I find it interesting to use contactless technology for handling guest complaints.

Habits

HAB1 I feel comfortable with contactless technology.

HAB2 I have already used contactless technology to interact with guests.

HAB3 I often use contactless technology applications in my work/outside work.

Intention

INT1 I have the intention to use contactless technology in my hotel for better guest experience.

INT2 I have the intention to use contactless technology routinely for improving confidence among guests.

INT3 I have the intention to use contactless technology when necessary to provide any information to the guest.

INT4 I would use contactless technology if I receive the necessary technical assistance.

Source: Author's own work.

Table 1.2. Demographic characteristics of the respondents (n=93).

Characteristics	Percentage	Number
Gender		
Male	73.8	69
Female	26.2	24
Designation		
Executive level	15.4	14
Managerial level	35.4	33
Supervisory level	21.5	20
Operational level	26.2	24
Owner	1	1
Department		
Food production	30.6	28
F&B service	21.2	20
Accommodation operation	23.6	22
Front office	9.6	9
Human resources	8.6	8
Sales and marketing	6.4	6

Continued

Table 1.2. Continued

Characteristics	Percentage	Number
Category of your establishment		
5 star	78.5	73
4 star	13.8	13
3 star	4.7	4
2 star	1.5	1
1 star	1.5	1
Total experience		
2–5 years	43.1	40
5–10 years	23.1	21
10–15 years	16.9	16
15 years and above	16.9	16
Age group		
25–30	50.8	47
30–35	18.5	17
35–40	16.9	16
40+	13.8	13
Highest qualification		
Simple graduation	10.8	10
Diploma from FCI	3.1	3
Degree in hotel management	53.8	50
Certificate course	4.6	4
Master's in hotel management	27.7	26

Source: Author's own work.

Table 1.3. Implementation status of contactless technology in hotels.

Status	Percentage	Number
Already implemented	47.7	44
In the process of implementation	26.2	24
Will implement within 6 months	3	3
Not yet decided	23.1	21

Source: Author's own work.

Sampling size

Hotel staff of various hotels in Amritsar Punjab were selected. The questionnaire was distributed online using Google forms.

Data analysis

Table 1.3 shows that hotels in Amritsar are well aware of contactless technology and are in the process of implementing it.

Table 1.4. Potential barriers that exist in the implementation of such technology.

Options	Percentage	Numbers
Limited acceptance by staff	18.3	17
Technical limitations	26.2	24
Security concerns	22	20
Awareness of technology	10.2	9
Increase in cost	8.3	8
Low transaction limit for payments	15	14

Source: Author's own work.

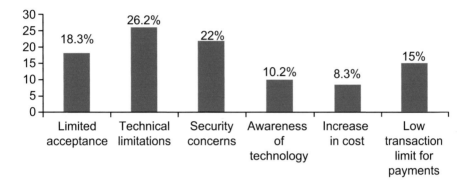

Fig. 1.1. Potential barriers to the implementation of contactless technology.
Source: Author's own work.

By using descriptive analysis, it was determined that all questions are over the midpoint (3.5). This result, shown in Table 1.6, shows that there is the acceptance of contactless technology in terms of its 'perceived usefulness' and 'perceived ease of use'. Also, variables such as intention, habit and compatibility are found to be in the high level of acceptance.

For analysing and measuring internal consistency among questions we have used Cronbach's alpha test (Glen, 2021). It was developed by Lee Cronbach in 1951. The multiple questions under the Likert scale are checked by Cronbach's alpha for their reliability. It is used to measure the latent variables such as habit, intention, compatibility, attitude etc. The results tell us how closely test items are related to each other in a group.

Concerning reliability of the questions asked, the reliability test (Table 1.5) indicates the alpha coefficient value is 0.930, which indicates that the instrument was reliable. There was a total of 26 questions asked for six variables. The results of the study revealed that intention and attitude are the major variables that influence the implementation of contactless technology.

Limitations of the Study

The results of our research are subject to some limitations. First, due to the ongoing pandemic, the hospitality industry is experiencing low staff numbers due to low business. The availability of staff to respond was a challenge and it was not possible to get a response from all departments of the hotels. Secondly, our work takes basic variables for the study. It is proposed that for future studies more variables, such as facilitators contributing to the acceptance of technology, may be used to improve the predictive power of the theoretical model.

Table 1.5. Analysis of the data obtained through Cronbach's alpha with average and variance.

Variables	Average	Variance	Cronbach's alpha
Perceived usefulness			0.965
PU1	4.95	3.55	
PU2	5.00	3.57	
PU3	4.78	3.78	
PU4	5.16	3.62	
PU5	5.03	2.97	
PU6	4.88	3.76	
Perceived ease of use			
PEU1	5.18	3.52	0.958
PEU2	5.00	3.57	
PEU3	5.00	3.59	
PEU4	4.85	3.72	
PEU5	5.00	3.46	
Attitude			
ATD1	5.23	3.31	0.942
ATD2	4.96	3.45	
ATD3	4.99	3.79	
ATD4	4.81	3.46	
Compatibility			
COMP1	5.02	3.91	0.931
COMP2	4.94	3.69	
COMP3	5.10	3.35	
COMP4	4.88	3.93	
Habit			
HAB1	5.13	3.50	0.850
HAB2	4.35	4.41	
HAB3	4.56	4.23	
Intention			
INT1	4.98	3.67	0.935
INT2	5.02	3.24	
INT3	4.91	3.82	
INT4	5.05	3.33	

Source: Author's own work.

Conclusion

Contactless technology is increasingly seen as an efficient way of building confidence among both guests and staff by maintaining social distancing and providing a safe environment in hotels. It is important to acknowledge that contactless technology is the new normal in the hotel industry and is becoming an essential part of upgrading systems, and it will remain part of the integrated support system for daily operations. Hotel employees are expected to accept contactless technology for its successful implementation. The prominent barriers (Fig. 1.1) to the implementation of contactless technology (Table 1.4) are technical limitations and security concerns.

References

Alsamydai, M.J. (2014) Adaptation of the technology acceptance model (TAM) to the use of mobile banking services. *International Review of Management and Business Research* 3(4), 2039.

Amrit (2021) What are contactless hotels? Shoocal. Available at: https://www.shoocal.com/blog/what-are-contactless-hotels (accessed 29 June 2021).

Glen, S. (2021) *Probability and Statistics Topic Index from Statistics*. HowTo.com: elementary statistics for the rest of us. Available at: https://www.statisticshowto.com/probability-and-statistics/ (accessed 1 February 2023).

Hassan, M., Kazmi, S.S.A.S. and Padlee, S.F. (2019) Technology acceptance model (TAM) and dynamics of online purchase adaptability. *International Journal of Recent Technology and Engineering* 8(1), 390–402.

Koontz, H. (2010) *Essentials of Management*. Tata McGraw-Hill Education.

Le, P.T. (2015) Human Resources Development: Induction Programs-Difficulties, Impacts and Solutions. Available at: https://www.theseus.fi/handle/10024/103185 (accessed 29 December 2022).

Sanad, H.M. (2014) Measuring consumers attitudes towards banking services offered by Iraqi public and private. *International Journal of Business, Management & Research* 107–115.

Silva, P. (2015) Davis' technology acceptance model (TAM) (1989). In: Al-Sugri, M.N. (Ed.) *Information Seeking Behavior and Technology Adoption: Theories and Trends*. IGI Global, pp. 205–219.

Sondhi, N. (2017) Segmenting & profiling the deflecting customer: understanding shopping cart abandonment. *Procedia Computer Science* 122(2), 392–399. DOI: 10.1016/j.procs.2017.11.385.

Sorell, M. (2020) Touchless tech: how hotels are preparing for a post-COVID guest experience. Phocuswire. Available at: https://www.phocuswire.com/contactless-technology-solutions-hotels-covid-19 (accessed 28 June 2021).

Venkatesh, V. and Davis, F.D. (2000) A theoretical extension of the technology acceptance model: four longitudinal field studies. *Management Science* 46(2), 186–204. DOI: 10.1287/mnsc.46.2.186.11926.

2 Increasing Tourism Resilience with Digital Engagement in the Hotel Industry

Rekha Maitra[1]* and Bindu Roy[2]

[1]Department of Travel and Tourism Management, DAV Centenary College, Faridabad, India; [2]Department of Commerce, DAV Centenary College, Faridabad, India

Abstract

This research paper aims to address the role of digital engagement in regaining customers' and employees' trust, and increasing the tourism industry's resilience in the wake of the COVID-19 pandemic. The impact of the pandemic has been felt by all countries around the globe in varying degrees. According to *The Times* (2020), the Indian economy suffered a setback of USD 1 trillion due to the lockdown of factories and businesses, suspended flights, halted trains, and restricted movement of vehicles and people.

The tourism industry, which has always been susceptible to various types of crises, has also felt the impact of the pandemic. The Indian hotel industry had estimated losses of more than USD 17 million in 2020–21. After the partial lifting of the lockdown, the hospitality industry opened its doors to welcome back guests with minimal human contact. Digitalization was perceived as a novelty before the pandemic, but it has now emerged as a necessity. Digital-driven artificial intelligence tools and big-data analytics have benefitted many industries. Reservations, check-in, check-out, rooms, food experiences, conferencing and delivery are handled seamlessly by hotels with digital engagements. Digitalization has become a facilitator for implementing stringent social distancing criteria and driving redefined customer experience.

Introduction

In 2020, the world populace was impacted by the COVID-19 pandemic. The challenge of saving human life resulted in developments in medical infrastructure and the advancement of the health emergency system. The World Health Organization (WHO) advised putting high-alert warnings on travelling to avoid disease transmission (Kaushik *et al.*, 2020). The disturbing impact of the pandemic was felt worldwide, leaving many people unemployed. The research study of Chen and Chen (2021) discussed the devastating effect of the pandemic on tourism and hospitality in Taiwan, which resulted in recession and sabbatical leave for employees. Job security and organizations were directly impacted. According to Dev and Sengupta (2020), the worsening situation paralysed the Indian economy with an unprecedented lockdown. The demand-and-supply chain disruption impacted the hospitality industry; as people stopped visiting hotels and restaurants to safeguard themselves, there was no revenue; hence, employees were made redundant. They further emphasized the grim situation of jobs and livelihoods being at stake. The closing of state and country borders impacted the labour supply in the urban areas of India. The collapse of supply mechanisms and disruption were felt in all sectors.

*Corresponding author: rekhavmaitra@gmail.com

© CAB International 2023. *Technology and Social Transformations in Hospitality, Tourism and Gastronomy: South Asia Perspectives* (eds S. Sharma and S. Bhartiya)
DOI: 10.1079/9781800621244.0002

A tragic situation in the tourism industry resulted in the adoption of social distancing and contactless digital technology. The study of Shapoval et al. (2021) focused on the health crisis of the hospitality industry in the USA, Israel and Sweden. These leaders focused on handling the COVID crisis through the lens of social systems theory.

Sharma et al. (2021) highlighted the four significant factors for enhancing tourism resilience, i.e. government response, digital innovation, local belongingness, and consumer and employee confidence.

Four prominent factors for building resilience in the industry are, we argue: using such inclusive resilience, the tourism industry may transform into a new global economic order characterized by sustainable tourism; society's wellbeing; climate action; and the involvement of local communities. We also offer directions for future research in the area.

This statement is further reinforced by the study of Madhukar and Sharma (2019), who discussed the significant role of advanced digitalization in enhancing the tourism industry's profitability. Digital information has been instrumental in designing dynamic pricing for hotels during the low and high seasons. Advanced technologies, i.e. artificial intelligence and big-data analytics, have helped maintain a more extensive database of customers. Adoption of digitalization promotes tourism products, enhances their accessibility, and makes the products visible and saleable via sales to potential customers, i.e. tourists, travel agents and tour operators. An empirical study on inter-organizational systems in developing resilience and agility was carried out by Mandal and Dubey (2021). Their investigation highlighted the prominent influence of Apple's iOS system for integration, collaboration and coordination on the development of tourism supply chain agility and resilience.

A study by Mandal (2019) discovered the regulating role of technology orientation (TO) on the information technology (IT) capabilities, outside-in and inside-out, in the development of tourism supply chain agility and resilience. Furthermore, Mandal and Saravanan (2019) discussed the significant influence of environmental, supply chain and learning orientations as significant tourism enablers. Although the effect of entrepreneurial and digital orientations was insignificant, this had positive path coefficients.

For increasing tourism resilience, digital adoption was a significant step. Gretzel and Scarpino-Johns (2018) focus on intelligent destinations and destination-resilience concepts. Their study offers insight into smart tourism destinations with resilient infrastructure to ensure seamless services. Gore et al. (2020) deliberated on the efficient utilization of technological road mapping, which can be helpful in co-creating sustainable tourism destinations for the future. Nuryyev et al. (2020) investigated the intention to adopt cryptocurrency payments in small and medium-sized enterprises in tourism and hospitality. Structural equation modelling was used to examine cryptocurrency's internal and external factors. Maitra (2021) further reinforced digital adoption and analysed digital implementation in the hotel industry. She deliberated that digital, robotic infrastructure and tech appliances adoption enhanced the accessibility of products and helped extend contactless services, i.e. sensory dispensers for emitting sanitizers and recording body temperature. On digital engagement, Maitra and Shukla (2022) discussed the pivotal role of digital-driven tools like artificial intelligence and big-data analytics, concluding that they were useful in business sectors: reservations, check-in, check-out, rooms, food service and delivery. Digitalization is enacted as a facilitator to embrace advancements.

Literature Review

An extensive literature review focused on the negative impacts of COVID-19 and how digitalization became a lifesaver for the industry.

Research Methodology

The research paper analyses digital engagement in building the resilience of hotel operators. A questionnaire was distributed to hoteliers to assess the implementation of digital in their daily operations for keeping staff and customers safe. Primary-data analysis was carried out with demographic profiling of gender, age and income group. The hypotheses were framed and digital adoption acceptance was judged. Various changes in standard operating procedures of hotels and resorts were judged based on frequency and percentage. An independent t-test was applied to the first hypothesis. The second hypothesis of ensuring the safety of guests through technological advancements was tested through Mean, and the third hypothesis was judged with an ANOVA test.

Data Analysis

It is essential to collect primary and secondary data to analyse the acceptability of new technological trends in the hotel industry post-pandemic. The primary data is collected from the hotel visitors to assist the researchers in judging the application of technological advancements to reduce the impact of COVID-19 in the hospitality industry.

Section A

Analysis of primary data

In the NCR region, 135 respondents were selected to analyse the data regarding demographic profiles and various technological changes adopted by the hospitality industry. Out of these 135, the data collected from 120 respondents were found to be suitable for data analysis. These responses were collected from Faridabad, Ghaziabad, Noida, Gurugram and New Delhi. Out of 120, nearly 60% of respondents had recently visited a hotel or resort after lockdown; 30% had not visited, while the rest, 10%, had visited virtually.

Analysis of demographic profiles of the respondents

The demographic profiles of the respondents are discussed below.

Gender

The gender profile of the visitors is categorized into two: male and female. Table 2.1 presents the gender profile of 120 visitors.

Age group

The age group profile of the visitors is categorized into five: 20–29 years, 30–39 years, 40–49 years, 50–59 years and 60–69 years. Table 2.2 presents the age group profile of 120 visitors.

Employment status

The employment status of the visitors is categorized into four: employed full time, employed part-time, self-employed, and student. Table 2.3 presents the employment status of 120 visitors.

Analysis of the technological changes adopted by hotels/resorts

Table 2.4 presents the number of visitors who have noticed any new changes in the hotels/resorts post-COVID-19.

It is evident from Table 2.4 that in the total sample of 120 visitors, 89 (74.2%) have noticed new technological changes that the hotels and resorts have adopted, while 10 have not noticed any changes. More than 20

Table 2.1. Gender profile.

Gender	Frequency	Percentage
Male	54	45
Female	66	55
Total	120	100

Source: Author's own work.

Table 2.2. Age group profile.

Age groups	Frequency	Percentage
20–29 years	61	50.83
30–39 years	20	16.67
40–49 years	25	20.83
50–59 years	11	9.17
60–69 years	03	2.5
Total	120	100

Source: Author's own work.

Table 2.3. Employment status.

Employment status	Frequency	Percentage
Employed full-time	52	43.5
Employed part-time	8	6.5
Self-employed	12	9.7
Student	48	40.3
Total	120	100

Source: Author's own work.

Table 2.4. Acceptance of digital adoption.

Acceptance of new changes in hotels	Frequency	Percentage
Yes	89	74.2
No	10	8.1
Maybe	21	17.7
Total	120	100

Source: Author's own work.

Table 2.5. Various changes in hotels and resorts.

New changes	Frequency	Percentage
Technological advancements	62	51.6
Digital transaction	77	64.5
Fully sanitized area	100	83.9
Hands-free sanitizer dispensers	87	72.6
Social distancing	77	64.5
Display of clean certification	43	35.5
Use of robots for cleaning/serving/cooking	10	8.1
Digital transactions	77	64.5
Any other	17	14.5

Source: Author's own work.

respondents either have not noticed any technological changes or are not aware of them. Thus, the data depict a higher percentage of respondents who have accepted that the hotels or resorts have adopted technological changes in the hospitality sector.

New changes in hotels and resorts after COVID-19

Table 2.5 shows the list of changes adopted by hotels and resorts after COVID-19.

It is revealed in Table 2.5 that the maximum percentage of respondents, i.e. 100 (83.9%), found thoroughly sanitized areas in hotels and resorts after COVID-19. Around 72.6% of respondents have seen the hotel/resort staff using hands-free sanitizer dispensers. The hotels and resorts follow digital transactions and social distancing protocols to ensure that customers are secure from infections. The hotels and resorts also use various digital technologies, like artificial

intelligence, augmented reality and virtual tours. Nevertheless, robotics adoption in cooking, serving or cleaning is still not very popular in hotels, as it requires much maintenance. It was realized that machines and digital might replace humans, but they cannot replace the human touch and personalization.

Hypothesis of the study

1. There is no significant difference in visitors' perceptions regarding the role of technological advancements in hotels based on gender.
2. There is no significant difference in the perceptions of various visitors of different age groups regarding hotel management initiatives to keep guests safe from COVID.
3. There is no significant difference in visitors' perceptions of acceptance and ease of use of digital technology in the hospitality sector based on employment status.

Table 2.6. Independent t-test.

Role of technological advancements in hotels	Mean		t-Test	DF	p-value	Remarks
	Male (n=54)	Female (n=66)				
Helpful in following safety protocols in hotels	4.6	4.2	1.89	118	0.87	No significant difference exists
Helpful in making minimal contact during check-in and check-out of guests in hotels	4.5	4.4	1.11	118	0.95	No significant difference exists
Helpful in creating a healthy and hygienic environment in hotels	4.1	4.0	0.53	118	0.59	No significant difference exists

Source: Author's own work.

Section B

Data analysis and hypothesis testing

Findings of first hypothesis

There is no significant difference in visitors' perceptions regarding the role of technological advancements in hotels based on gender.

Interpretation

Table 2.6 shows that there is no significant difference in the perceptions of males and females regarding the role of technological advancements in hotels based on gender, as the results show that the p-value of the t-statistic is 0.87 in case 1, 0.95 in case 2 and 0.59 in case 3, and all the p-values are higher than 0.05 at the 5% level of significance.

Hence, with 95% confidence in the null hypothesis regarding following hotel safety protocols, making minimal contact during check-in and check-out of guests and creating a healthy and hygienic environment, the perceptions of male and female respondents can be accepted. Thus, it can be concluded from the results of an independent sample t-test that both males and females accept that digital implementation in hotels with proper COVID-19 safety protocols would be beneficial for the hospitality sector in future.

Findings of second hypothesis

There is no significant difference in the perceptions of various visitors of different age groups regarding hotel management initiatives to keep guests safe from COVID.

As there are no significant variations in the perceptions of various visitors of different age groups, the researchers have considered only the mean value as per 5 points of the Likert scale, rating by: 1. strongly disagree; 2. disagree; 3. cannot say; 4. agree; and 5. strongly agree. The findings of the data analysis are shown in Table 2.7.

Interpretation

1. Eight out of 12 steps taken by the hotel management to keep guests safe from COVID were acceptable by all the respondents.
2. More than 75% of respondents agreed that digital transactions; URL-based links; innovative room access system; contactless check-in and check-out; QR code for check-in and check-out, menu and other services; UV rays box to disinfect the necessary items; and new healthy, hygienic and safety protocols to protect against COVID should be initiated by the hotel authority to maintain the safety and security of their guests during the pandemic.

Table 2.7. Assuring the safety of guests through technological advancements.

Statements regarding steps to keep guests safe by the hotel management through technological advancements	Mean
Digital payment/transactions	4.83
URL-based links/apps/kiosks for contactless service	4.46
Virtual display of product	3.53
Smart room access system/convenient and secure room key option	4.53
Contactless dispensers, sanitizing machine and thermal screening machine	4.1
Face scanner/retina scanner/skull scanner	3.35
Car and luggage sanitizing machine	2.61
Robots for serving, cooking, delivering laundry and distributing housekeeping supplies	3.46
Contactless check-in and check-out	4.55
QR code check-in check-out/menu/any other service	4.74
UV rays box to disinfect mobiles, keyrings, wallets, belts, etc.	4.93
New health, hygiene and safety protocols to protect against COVID-19	4.38

Source: Author's own work.

3. Almost 50% of respondents were neutral about the virtual display of products, usage of face and retina scanners, and utilizing robots for cleaning, cooking, serving food and other tasks to maximize the contactless services for the welfare of guests in hotels.
4. Only 20% of respondents disagreed with the initial steps taken by the hospitality sector to use car- and luggage-sanitizing machines for the health and safety of their guests.

Findings of third hypothesis

There is no significant difference in visitors' perceptions of acceptance and ease of use of digital technology in the hospitality sector based on employment status.

Interpretation

Table 2.8 represents the results of the F-test in one-way ANOVA. As shown in Table 2.8, the *p*-value (sig. value) of the F-statistic is less than 5% significance. Hence, with a 95% confidence level, the null hypothesis cannot be accepted. Thus, it can be concluded from the results that perceptions of respondents of different employment categories are not the same. There are differences in perceptions regarding the adoption

and implementation of digital advancements in the hospitality sector in the post-pandemic period, especially in India; they do not accept that the Indian hospitality sector can survive easily for a long time with high levels of technology.

Conclusion

This research paper addresses the positive impact of digitalization in managing COVID-19 safety protocols by employing new and robust applications, which have enhanced the opportunities for the hotel industry and increased its resilience. The research also reveals the benefits of a digital-driven environment in maintaining safety protocols. The paper offers insights of hoteliers in understanding the new normal with safety protocols during mandated social distancing.

The study highlights the role of big-data analytics in maintaining the customers', employees', partners' and hotels' quarantine-related data. It recommends practical solutions for hoteliers in optimizing digital utilization and synthesizing digital usage in maintaining social distancing norms. In an effort to survive, the hospitality industry has embraced technological advancements such as online travel agents,

Table 2.8. ANOVA test.

Acceptance and survival of technological advancements in the hospitality sector	Employment status			F-statistic (*p*-value)	Remarks
	Employed (mean)	Not employed (mean)	Self-employed (mean)		
Comfortably accepted by the guests in the post-pandemicera	4.432	4.679	4.167	8.041 (0.000)	Significant difference exists
Easily survive with high digital implementation in India	4.640	4.748	4.185	11.339 (0.000)	Significant difference exists

Source: Author's own work.

smartphones and personal digital assistance (PDA), and transforming how interactions occur. Marriott, Hilton, IHG and Accor utilize artificial intelligence, robotics and big data. The revamped digital-oriented business model offers many possibilities to develop and nurture relationships with all stakeholders. Technological advancements can be a source of revamping the business and support to boost the economy of India.

In the post-COVID-19 phase, digital use in the service sector in India is rising gradually. The new normal has been boosted by enhancing the visibility of brands on the digital platform. The tourism and hospitality sectors are working on the digital platform. The industry has adopted the digital platform for enhancing the visibility of its product line and will continue to do so in the future.

References

Chen, C.-L. and Chen, M.-H. (2021) Hospitality industry employees' intention to stay in their job after the COVID-19 pandemic. *Administrative Sciences* 11(4), 144. DOI: 10.3390/admsci11040144.

Dev, S.M. and Sengupta, R. (2020) *Covid-19: Impact on the Indian Economy*. Indira Gandhi Institute of Development Research, Mumbai.

Gore, S., Borde, N. and Desai, P.H. (2020) Assessment of technology strategies for sustainable tourism planning. *Foresight* 23(2), 172–187. DOI: 10.1108/FS-02-2020-0006.

Gretzel, U. and Scarpino-Johns, M. (2018) Destination resilience and smart tourism destinations. *Tourism Review International* 22(3), 263–276. DOI: 10.3727/154427218X15369305779065.

Kaushik, S., Kaushik, S., Sharma, Y., Kumar, R. and Yadav, J.P. (2020) The Indian perspective of COVID-19 outbreak. *Virusdisease* 31(2), 146–153. DOI: 10.1007/s13337-020-00587-x.

Madhukar, V. and Sharma, D. (2019) The role of information technology applications in profitability. *Worldwide Hospitality and Tourism Themes* 11(4), 429–437. DOI: 10.1108/WHATT-04-2019-0025.

Maitra, R. (2021) Adoption and implementation of digital transformation for the sustainability of tourism and hospitality business in India. *Journal of Services Research* 21(1).

Maitra, R. and Shukla, D. (2022) Covid-19 and technology internventions: an exploratory study of the Indian hospitality industry. Available at: http://ihmahmedabad.com/download/others/journal%20index_2022_vol4_issue1/403.pdf (accessed 10 December 2022).

Mandal, S. (2019) Exploring the influence of IT capabilities on agility and resilience in tourism: moderating role of digital orientation. *Journal of Hospitality and Tourism Technology* 10(3), 401–414.

Mandal, S. and Dubey, R.K. (2021) An empirical investigation is the effect of inter-organizational systems appropriation in agility and resilience development. *Benchmarking: An International Journal* 28(9), 2656–2681. DOI: 10.1108/BIJ-10-2020-0542.

Mandal, S. and Saravanan, D. (2019) Exploring the influence of strategic orientations on tourism supply chain agility and resilience: an empirical investigation. *Tourism Planning & Development* 16(6), 612–636. DOI: 10.1080/21568316.2018.1561506.

Nuryyev, G., Wang, Y.P., Achyldurdyyeva, J., Jaw, B.S., Yeh, Y.S. *et al.* (2020) Blockchain technology adoption behavior and sustainability of the business in tourism and hospitality SMEs: an empirical study. *Sustainability* 12(3), 1256. DOI: 10.3390/su12031256.

Shapoval, V., Hägglund, P., Pizam, A., Abraham, V., Carlbäck, M. *et al.* (2021) Using social systems theory, the COVID-19 pandemic effects on the hospitality industry: a multi-country comparison. *International Journal of Hospitality Management* 94, 102813. DOI: 10.1016/j.ijhm.2020.102813.

Sharma, G.D., Thomas, A. and Paul, J. (2021) Reviving tourism industry post-COVID-19: a resilience-based framework. *Tourism Management Perspectives* 37, 100786. DOI: 10.1016/j.tmp.2020.100786.

The Times (2020) https://timesofindia.indiatimes.com/world/us/trump-presses-for-1-trillion-stimulus-as-us-coronavirus-deaths-cross-100/articleshow/74683320.cms (accessed 13 February 2023).

3 The Role of Influencers in Destination Marketing through Instagram Social Platform

Zahra Nadalipour[1]*, Afsheen Hassan[2], Shivam Bhartiya[3] and Fatemeh Shah Hosseini[1]

[1]*University of Science and Culture, Tehran, Iran;* [2]*Superior University, Lahore, Pakistan;* [3]*Central University of Karnataka, Kalaburagi, India*

Abstract

Today, social media has considerably affected all social and economic aspects of our lives. Marketing is one of the fields which has significantly evolved through applying the power of virtual networks and social platforms, particularly marketing of tourism and travel products. Social platforms such as Instagram, by using their capabilities in sharing photos and video clips, have played an effective role in promoting tourist destinations. On the other hand, having a large number of followers, influencers on social platforms have a huge impact on tourists' decision-making patterns. Thus, studying how social platforms affect marketing activities is vital to survival in today's competitive environment. In this regard, the present research aims to study the role of social platform influencers in marketing tourist destinations, as well as identify appropriate criteria in selecting influencers by marketers. Therefore, the Instagram platform was targeted as the case. A series of semi-structured, in-depth interviews took place to gather the required data, which were analysed using the Thematic Analysis method. A sample of nine experts was taken from a population of specialists in the fields of marketing, tourism, media and content production. Finally, extracted themes were classified into six groups including: criteria to select influencers by tourism marketers; shared content; destination promotion; prerequisites for tourism businesses; influencer–business interactions; and potential of the Instagram platform. In turn, sub-themes were extracted and described in detail. The findings of the present study have several practical implications for destination marketers, particularly for those who are active in the field of digital marketing, as well as influencers and individuals seeking to attract audiences and increase their credibility on social media.

Introduction

The viral nature of social media has provided brand managers with significant opportunities to increase positive interactions through word-of-mouth advertising (Killian and McManus, 2015). Keller and Fay (2016), cited in Gretzel (2018), refer to influencers as daily consumers who are almost certain to seek out information and share ideas, information and recommendations with others through volunteering their opinions about products and services that they are excited about which are then adopted by others because of their knowledge, advice and insight. Social media influencers are 'vocational, sustained and highly branded social media stars' who 'exert influence over a large pool of potential customers' (Abidin, 2018; as cited in Femenia-Serra and Gretzel, 2020, p. 66). They are a new type of online

*Corresponding author: z.nadalipour@usc.ac.ir

DOI: 10.1079/9781800621244.0003

opinion leader and brand endorser (Freberg *et al.*, 2011) with great power to influence their followers, which has made them the focus of influencer marketing strategy (De Veirman *et al.*, 2017; Bokunewicz and Shulman, 2017) (ibid.). One of the most important functions of social networks is the formation of electronic verbal marketing among the members, which is considered a major function of such networks. Social networks, particularly those with capabilities in sharing photos and videos, such as Instagram, have played a vital role in promoting tourist destinations by changing the type of communications. Instagram is an American photo- and video-sharing social networking service founded by Kevin Systrom and Mike Krieger in 2010. Focusing on visual communication, this social platform can help better promote products and services. The costs associated with marketing activities are significantly reduced by using this platform.

The purpose of the present research is to study the role of Instagram influencers in marketing tourist destinations. It also aims to identify appropriate criteria in selecting influencers by marketers. In this regard, influencers' characteristics, as well as factors contributing to the selection of influencers, have been studied. In the forthcoming sections, relevant literature is reviewed by focusing on previous studies. Afterwards, the methodology of the study is addressed by analysing the findings and results. Finally, the conclusion and discussion, as well as the limitations and recommendations for future research, are presented.

Literature Review

Several studies have confirmed the role of social media in the travel and tourism decision process. According to Leung *et al.* (2013), from 2007 to 2011, travel and tourism studies mainly focused on the use and impact of social media in the research phase of travellers' travel planning processes. On the other hand, supplier-centric studies have concentrated more closely on promotion, management and research functions rather than product distribution. From a consumer-centric perspective, for example, McCarthy *et al.* (2010), cited in Leung *et al.* (2013), studied the impact of social media on changing hotel customer preferences. Another

example from the same source is a study conducted by Fotis *et al.* (2011), which found the role of media in changing the way holiday plans were made by online users from Russia and the former Soviet Union republics had changed. On the other hand, regarding supplier-centric studies, an example cited in Leung *et al.*, 2013, is Pan *et al.*'s 2007 work, which indicated the effectiveness and implications of analysing blog entries in destination marketing. Leung *et al.*'s 2011 work is another example demonstrating the cost-effectiveness of monitoring travel blogs by destination marketers in order to recognize travellers' experiences (Leung *et al.*, 2013).

With regard to the impact of social media on destination branding, Lim *et al.* (2012) studied consumer perception of destination brands created by consumer-generated videos and destination marketing organizations' videos. They found that 'consumer-generated videos do not carry the same destination brand as destination marketer-generated videos' (p. 197). They also found that those videos created by the consumer have little positive impact on a destination brand. Regarding destination images, Stepchenkova and Zhan (2013), in their study, compared images of Peru collected from a DMO's site and from Flickr, a photo-sharing website. They identified statistical differences in several dimensions of these images by producing maps representing 'aggregated' projected and perceived images of Peru, and maps indicating the geographical distribution of the images.

With reference to better communication with the customer through social networks, Tussyadiah *et al.* (2011) cited in Leung *et al.*, 2013, argued that audiences will be more motivated to choose a given destination if they gain information about a place through user-generated content on social media. In the same vein, Sparks and Browning (2011) found that the probability of booking a hotel by customers is determined by valence, framing and inclusion of ratings in online reviews. Wang and Fesenmaier (2004), cited as above, also revealed that 'social media are useful for managing customer relations with their unique ability of attracting customers through in-depth, focused and member-generated content, engaging customers through social interactions, and retaining customers through relation building with other members' (Leung *et al.*, 2013, p. 4).

Recognizing customers' needs and wants, Dellarocas (2003) argued that social media provides extraordinary opportunities for tourism companies in order to understand and respond to consumer preferences. Online comments on social platforms such as Tripadvisor and Virtualtourist can be analysed by companies to better recognize customers' expectations and preferences (Leung *et al.*, 2013). On the other hand, regarding use of social platforms as marketing tools, Hay (2010) investigates the use of twittering from the perspectives of destination marketing organizations, hotels and the consumer. The findings revealed that twittering provides consumers with an opportunity to learn and share common experiences. Another study is Belias *et al.* (2017) work, which investigates how social media can act as a tool for acquiring knowledge and creating a collaborative environment in the case of the Greek tourism industry.

Considering studies in the area of influencer marketing, Gretzel (2018), in a book chapter titled 'Influencer marketing in travel and tourism', argued that 'Despite its prominence and practical significance, there is a lack of research that investigates the travel and tourism influencer marketing phenomenon'. However, one of the relevant studies to the present research is De Veirman *et al.* (2017). By focusing on Instagram, they studied the impact of number of followers and product divergence on brand attitude. The findings of their research revealed that Instagram influencers with large numbers of followers are found to be more likeable due to being more popular. They also found that 'only in limited cases, perceptions of popularity induced by the influencer's number of followers increase the influencer's perceived opinion leadership' (p. 1). In addition, following very few accounts by the influencer can negatively impact his/her likeability. It also was revealed that 'cooperating with influencers with high numbers of followers might not be the best marketing choice for promoting divergent products, as this decreases the brand's perceived uniqueness and consequently brand attitudes' (p. 1). In another study, featuring interviews with destination representatives, social media content analysis and relevant reported data, Femenia-Serra and Gretzel (2020) investigated the use of social media influencers by destination management organizations and the inner dynamics of influencer marketing for tourism destinations.

Moreover, using self-congruity theory, Xu (Rinka) and Pratt (2018) investigated social media influencers as endorsers to promote travel destinations, in a case of Chinese Generation Y. They found that 'social media influencers' endorser–consumer congruence positively contributes to visit intentions toward the endorsed destinations as does endorser–destination congruence' (p. 1). Gretzel (2018) raised the important question of how to conceptualize influence and how to formulate effective influencer campaigns. She also referred to the question of how consumers perceive travel and tourism social media influencers and what drives the persuasiveness of influencer messages. The present study has partly tried to find answers to these questions.

Methodology

Owing to the fact that the present study is an exploratory one in nature, a qualitative approach was adopted in conducting the research. Semi-structured, in-depth interviews therefore were applied to gathering the required data which were analysed later by using a thematic analysis approach. In this way, transcripts of interviews were read carefully. Then, initial coding was done using MAXQDA software and extracted codes were synthesized to create the basic themes. By applying a purposive approach and snowball sampling method, a sample of nine experts was taken from a population of specialists in the fields of marketing, tourism, media and content production. Sample size was determined based on achieving theoretical saturation. Regarding credibility (Lincoln *et al.*, 1985) of the research, since interviewees were experts with sound experience in the relevant fields, and also as the same interviewer conducted all interviews, it can be argued that there are no issues with the credibility of the research. With reference to the transferability (Lincoln *et al.*, 1985) of the research, this was considered as all stages of the research process are described in detail.

Findings

Table 3.1 demonstrates the interviewees' profiles including experience, education and job/

Table 3.1. Interviewees' profile.

Interviewee	Experience (year)	Education	Job/specialty
1	15	Master's	Restaurant front-of-house manager
2	8	Master's	Executive manager of tourism marketing corporations
3	18	Bachelor's	Hotel owner
4	10	Master's	Tourism influencer
5	10	Associate	Hotel influencer
6	20	Associate	Tourism agency manager
7	10	Master's	Tourism website content manager
8	5	Bachelor's	Tourism content producer
9	4	Bachelor's	Coffee shop manager

Source: Author's own work.

specialty. As noted before, nine experts in areas covering content production, tourism enterprises management and tourism influencers were selected and interviewed.

According to the answers of the interviewees, the coding in MXQDA software was done in terms of three steps: open coding, axial coding and selective coding. Afterwards, in order to better organize the codes in the software, extracted codes were categorized and the main themes were extracted. The main categories, such as criteria to select influencers by tourism marketers, shared content, destination promotion, prerequisites for tourism businesses, influencer–business interactions, and potential of Instagram were obtained. These categories are discussed in more detail. Fig. 3.1 demonstrates thematic map of the main themes and relevant codes.

Criteria to Select Influencers by Tourism Marketers

With regard to the findings of the research, 'criteria to select influencers by tourism marketers' was identified as one of the main themes based on ten extracted codes as can be seen in Table 3.2. These codes are: audience size/popularity, influencer genre, originality, lived experience, quality of expression, influencer relevancy to the tourism field, influencer personality, feeling intimacy and closeness with the influencer, influencer gender, and not being fake.

Audience size/popularity

'Micro-influencers' refer to users who have recently started working on a given social media platform, and their primary goal for content production is to attract the audience. These people are also less famous with a limited number of followers. The positive feature of micro-influencers is that they have a deeper connection with their followers, so they receive better feedback. As suggested by one of the influencers: 'When a person has a smaller audience, it will be very easy to talk to them' (5). Another interviewee also mentioned this point during the interview: 'It depends on how many followers he/she has. Sometimes, for example, number of followers is up to 4 or 5 digits. In this case, he/she can communicate more and be available; however, sometimes you cannot really expect to be able to communicate with him/her' (3).

On the other hand, macro-influencers are the most active and popular users, sometimes with more than 500,000 followers. From one expert's perspective: 'When choosing a type of influencer, it is very important what the purpose of the product is. Sometimes it is obvious who a micro is. For example, it starts with 500–600 followers and is growing, and the trust that exists between him/her and the followers is

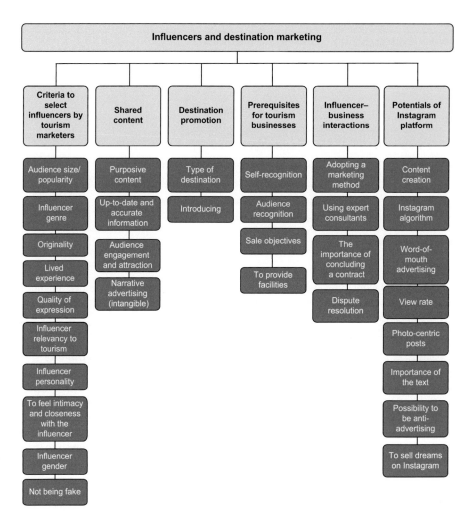

Fig. 3.1. Thematic map of the main themes.
Source: Author's own work.

very strong and closer; while in the case of macro-influencers, the number of followers is above 200,000 and his/her market is more public' (Belias *et al.*, 2017). However, according to the experts' opinion on the importance of the number of followers, half of the interviewees suggested that it is misleading to consider only this factor. They were of the opinion that the goal of the sale is more important: 'The worst type of selection is to consider only the number' (4). 'If the influence of the influencer is high, his/her audiences will also increase over time. In contrast, there may exist influencers who have a large number of followers, but their

followers are not real people' (9). 'According to an unwritten rule, although the number of followers is an important factor in gaining trust and popularity in cyberspace, there is no doubt that the quality of content is not necessarily related to the number of followers. There are also many ways to increase the number of audiences that are not related to the quality of the content' (7). The other half responded to the question about the importance of the number of followers as follows: 'As you know, the number of followers is the first thing you see after entering each page, so the first and easiest way to make an initial judgement is to look at the number of

Table 3.2. Criteria to select influencers by tourism marketers and related codes.

Theme	Codes	Frequency
Criteria to select influencers by tourism marketers	Audience size/popularity	29
	Influencer genre	21
	Originality	8
	Lived experience	17
	Quality of expression	22
	Influencer relevancy to the tourism field	11
	Influencer personality	15
	To feel intimacy and closeness with the influencer	11
	Influencer gender	12
	Not being fake	11

Source: Author's own work.

followers and to measure a person's popularity in this way' (8). 'In any case, no matter we think that the number of audiences is not important and the quality of the audience will have a greater impact on a brand, because we must also give the right to the advertiser' (5). From the audience perspective, one interviewee argued: 'Merely having a large number of followers is not a criterion for choosing and following, but if two influencers operate in exactly one area (e.g. food tourism), a high number of followers can indicate the reliability of the influencer and impact whether or not to follow' (2).

Generally, it was revealed the first step in choosing an influencer is usually to consider the number of followers. On the other hand, the popularity of an influencer is one of his/her most critical features. Popularity includes several criteria such as a large following, good interaction, reputation, and high impact. Intangible popularity is a pushing factor which forces users to follow his/her favourite influencer. The features such as being honest, proper public relations, being responsive and intimate, having real followers etc. make a person popular. As one interviewee suggested: 'The more an influencer contacts with the audience, the higher would be his/her popularity' (8). 'Friendship is more important than anything else in a blogger's popularity. Being cheerful attracts the attention of others and increases the effect of words on the audience. The influencer should always remember that a powerful way

to get the audience's attention and persuasion is jocundity' (5). Another contributory factor to the popularity of an influencer is its responsiveness. In this regard, one interviewee stated that: 'I have always preferred those influencers who are responsive despite being busy. This makes the position of the influencer in the mind ten times higher' (3). Using a popular influencer as a destination ambassador greatly helps in branding the destination image and in paving the way for actors engaging in destination marketing.

Influencer genre

The genre of influencers in this research means having a profession in a specific field (not just tourism) or being well known, regardless of having a specific specialty. In this regard, one of interviewees argued: 'Due to my personal experience, I see that a person who produces content in a specialized field, especially tourism, even if he/she is not an expert in that field, but with a more colourful content, can be more attractive than a person who presents his/her content in a more scientific and specialized way' (5). Another interviewee was of the opinion that 'expertise is the last step to gaining fame in cyberspace' (6). However, another pointed out that '...criteria vary for individuals. Sometimes it is important to use one's experiences or familiarity with tourism destinations' (9). 'An influencer defines a personality for his/herself and has a special genre. If you know your audience perfectly, then you can choose right. You need to know who you want to influence' (4). 'I prefer it not to be too general; rather, be specific, for example food influencer. For example, X [refers to one influencer] started a specialized tour of local foods. This person knew everything in this regard, and made a business' (2).

What can be concluded from most of the interviewees' opinions is that although specialized influencers have been more successful in attracting audiences, because the audiences more likely follow the individual based on their content, the audiences also pay more attention to the more colourful and glamorous content offered by ordinary influencers. Therefore, if it is only about visibility and popularity, marketing through famous people who produce more glamorous content is probably more successful.

Originality

Originality also greatly increases an influencer's influence and his/her chance to be selected and followed. According to one of the interviewees, 'These are interconnected chains. When you want your words to be effective and you want to act positively and not to be fake, naturally you have to have an identity which is something inherent' (1). Generally, from the perspective of experts and audiences, experience, stable personality, avoiding multitasking or not leaping from subject to subject, as well as a deep understanding of a certain context, are the signs of originality for an influencer.

Lived experience

Another theme frequently mentioned in interviews was influencers' experiences and their encounter with real events: 'Another feature that is important to me is influencers' lived experience; for example, maybe he/she graduates from university just today, and claims tomorrow that I am an influencer in this field, without any practical or relevant experience. Inversely, there are those influencers who have been travelling for years and have enough experience; so they enter Instagram space and present themselves' (2). The difference between experiencing and

not experiencing a situation is usually easily recognizable, so that audiences who have already experienced that situation will recognize a lack of real experience in the content shared by an influencer. Regarding the importance of experience in attracting followers, one of the interviewees expressed her opinion as follows: 'If he/she narrates to me the real experiences that took place there, and I could later experience the same thing that he/she had promised by narration, I will certainly become his/her loyal follower' (3). In addition, one of the interviewee's opinion as a hotelier was noteworthy: 'Behind every experience there is a thought, a satisfaction and a feeling. You should give meaning to the places and destinations, and if an influencer cannot do it, he/she must leave the influencer marketing' (3). According to some interviewees, it considerably impacts audiences' selection because it indicates that a given influencer is not fake and an imitator. One of the interviewees referred to the importance of the issue, particularly in destination marketing: 'When it comes to the travel and tourism, attending the destination and facing its attractions by influencers is one of the important factors that will affect the destination marketing' (7).

Quality of expression

With respect to the influencer's quality of expression and how he/she communicates with the audiences, the interviewees had various answers, which were similar. The quality of expression is crucial in influencing followers, as well as in being effective in marketing a tourist destination. One of the interviewees argued that: 'This is determined by their [influencers] personal brand. Having a humorous and witty tone usually does not work. Being dry and deadpan still does not work; rather, they should [be] friendly and enthusiastic' (4). In a similar way, another interviewee suggested: 'This depends on the type of content. Each content requires its own favourite way of expression. For sure, the ability to speak and present well is very important in attracting the audience' (6). 'I personally do not agree with being so formal. Of course, to some extent, it also depends on the type of audience and the type of blogger personality and prestige' (5). However, another interviewee has a moderate view: 'The balance between these two tones [formal and friendly] is important. Influencers' extreme emphasis on one single type can make the audience bored' (5). However, from a more comprehensive perspective, one interviewee had a different opinion: 'It depends on your target market. Sometimes you should be formal, sometimes more friendly. It cannot be said which one is better or more effective. It depends on the influencer and his/her followers' (Belias *et al.*, 2017). Another interviewee, active in the accommodation sector, referred to the *tone of voice* as a contributory factor to attract audiences: 'If tone of voice is not impressive, I cannot be absorbed [in] or believe what he/she is talking or writing about' (3). Confirming the above-mentioned argument, another expert referred to the relationship between tone of voice and audience type: 'Each tone and style of speech has its own audience. If one wants to convey the content to children, for example, he/she must use a narrative and childish tone. Communication with the adult audience also has its conditions. But in my opinion, each influencer leaves a mark on the audience with his/her unique tone. Influencers usually greet audiences with a special and repetitive tone, and the same tone is recorded in their mind (7).

Influencer relevance to the tourism field

In this study, relevance to the tourism field means whether it is better to use specialized travel- and tourism-related influencers in order to promote a destination or to use non-related but more famous influencers. Interestingly, a small number of interviewees agreed with the use of travel-related influencers, while in the opinion of other experts and even tourism-related influencers, the use of famous influencers would be more influential for destination marketing as they are more successful in producing attractive content and engaging audiences. 'I'm a related-influencer fan, but I also see influencers who are not acting in the field of tourism but they are successful, because a wide range of people are following them. These followers might also be interested in the tourism field' (2). According to Belias *et al.* (2017): 'A person with related knowledge can

help us better. He/she can promote a destination in a more professional and specialized way, but then again, famous influencers who have a lot of followers, might be more effective'. Most interviewees were of the opinion that travel- and tourism-related influencers are successful in introducing a destination rather than promoting it, since effective promotion requires producing compelling content which would be more successful.

Influencer personality

The influencer's personality was a code repeatedly mentioned in most of the interviewees' responses. Most of them suggested that to follow an influencer on the social network, they inevitably consider his/her personality. According to one interviewee: 'I look at personality traits; how acceptable he/she is. It is also affected by my personal feelings, but I try not to be overwhelmed. I try to see who we want to work with in terms of attitude and personality' (Belias *et al.*, 2017). Other interviewees put a lot of emphasis on the influencer's personality: 'The influencer introduces him/herself based on a particular behaviour or lifestyle which attracts his/her audience' (3). One of the influencers interviewed considered attributes such as self-confidence, tone, idea and personal signature to be important in following an influencer. It must be noted that, in this part, *personality* means being in accord with the accepted social norms and having the correct and appropriate position in the social networks.

To feel intimacy and closeness with the influencer

There must be a sense of intimacy and closeness with the influencer from the perspective of both personality and goal. Regarding the choice of destination, one of the interviewees argued: 'A successful influencer is one who brings you closer to the purpose of your trip. I myself choose someone who can involve me in the cultural context and the natural nature of the city and the place where I want to go'

(1). In this way, the issue of shared value was raised by one of the interviewees: 'If influencers have a better relationship with the common values of their followers, they can have a more lasting impact' (3). On the other hand, with regard to the selection of an influencer by a tourism company, several criteria, such as similarity of the two sides' thought and whether the content is real or unreal, have been emphasized by interviewees.

Influencer gender

One of the questions raised about influencers was about their gender, with most interviewees agreeing that females have a greater ability to attract audiences than males. For example: 'Females are better because they have a closer look at everything and can analyse and introduce in details' (2). 'Females are detail orientated. They are also more interested in sharing colourful and glazed content and pictures. They are more active and use Instagram more often than males' (8). But three interviewees believed that gender did not play a role in the selection of individuals and that the degree of ability of individuals depends on the type of content which is shared and on the purpose of the content: 'Since it was not common for females to travel alone until a few decades ago, their activities may have attracted more attention in social networks, but in general, why should there be a difference?' (7). 'Being an influencer is an issue that can be less dependent on gender because audiences are attracted to the abilities and other characteristics of influencers more than their gender' (9). 'In my opinion, gender does not matter if a correct and lasting result is desired; but if only getting attention and increasing sales are considered (perhaps not for sure), then the position of females might be better for success' (6).

Not being fake

One of the most important things that any stakeholder directly involved in the marketing of the destination should pay full attention to is being a real influencer. Because being real or 'not being fake' in all dimensions, both in the number of followers and the shared content, is very important in influencing audiences. However, the importance of not being fake in the number of followers is much more important than the type of content, since having unrealistic followers, especially for marketing purposes, is a big obstacle to achieving the goal. In fact, spending for an influencer with a fake audience is one of the biggest losses that can hit investors hard financially. As interviewed experts suggested, due to the vastness of cyberspace and the availability of information, the slightest mistake in sharing content would cause the unpopularity of an influencer and, as a result, cause the audience to distrust him/her and other content in the long run. 'When he/she wants to play a role, audiences gradually realize it and will be [lost]' (5). One of the interviewees who is a hotel owner also emphasized this issue: 'If I realize that his/her followers are fake I do not consider him/her to advertise my hotel' (3).

Shared Content

Another theme identified by extracted codes is *shared content*. Shared content on Instagram depends to a large extent on the influencer's genre. Such content includes a vast range of issues and it can or cannot pertain to the influencer's lifestyle. Influencers' marketing activities, for example, cover some part of this content. Extracted codes, based on which shared content theme was identified, are presented in Table 3.3.

Purposive content

Any shared content must have a specific purpose. As active users are looking for purposive content and, based on this, usually follow certain influencers, sharing content with a purposeful approach is crucial. In this vein, one expert is of the opinion that: 'Those operators using this platform [Instagram] would have a superior position than competitors. Thus, when it comes to the tourism field, if purposive and appropriate contents are produced, Instagram would be a critical context' (6). Referring to the purposeful activity of influencers, another

Table 3.3. Shared content and related codes.

Theme	Codes	Frequency
Shared content	Purposive content	18
	Up-to-date and accurate information	21
	Audience engagement and attraction	25
	Narrative advertising (intangible)	21

Source: Author's own work.

expert suggested: 'A tourism influencer should adopt acculturalization purpose for his/her page sharing it with the audiences' (5). What was frequently mentioned by interviewees is the lack of fine content and disregarding the concept, as well as more attention to the deceptive and almost unpurposeful contents. In regard to the harmony between appearance and concept, one interviewee argued: 'What is of the high value is the concept; I mean what concept we have and what concept we show. They should fit their texts, colours, photos etc. with a given concept' (3). Conclusively, influencers should reflect a certain purpose in terms of both appearance and content in order to increase their success.

Up-to-date and accurate information

Owing to the presence of a large number of users on Instagram, as well as free flow of information, sharing accurate and up-to-date information is of high importance. Considering the meaning of being up-to-date, one interviewee believes: 'Being up-to-date means not lagging behind the others, and when something becomes more trendy in any subject, it will be realized quickly; otherwise, the audience will be attracted to someone who has more information, and thus he/she loses the audience' (10). 'Being up-to-date shows that a person is really active. A literate person gives good information to his/her audience so that they are attracted to him/her. As for the accuracy of the information, if I want to say my opinion, usually a person lies to his/her own detriment, because his/her followers will investigate what he/she said. Someone who shares false information is not trustworthy' (5). In a similar way, another interviewee suggested: 'Honesty is very important because if the audience feels that the influencer is not honest enough or only produces content to advertise

and receive money, it will destroy the trust and influence on the audience. I myself did not follow many bloggers because of their dishonesty' (8). All participants agreed that marketing based on invalid or old information will fail.

Audience engagement and attraction

Even purposeful content is not effective unless it is attractive. Good content should engage audiences in what it is conveying. Features such as responsiveness, a sense of intimacy, a friendly tone of voice, attractive visual content etc. are effective in creating attention; however, there are no absolute criteria pertinent to attracting audiences, particularly in the tourism field where, besides the range of destinations, there are various types of tourists with diverse interests and expectations: 'You have different requests from customers of different categories and personas, and you cannot look at it comprehensively at all. Each category of customer has its own characteristics, interests and concerns... each influencer produces something that his/her customers like' (4). Another interviewee referred to one of the ways to engage an audience: 'I think that live video is more influential than photos, catalogues and texts. It engages the audience more, by providing a more tangible experience' (1). From a similar perspective, one of the interviewees described the importance of uploading photos in absorbing audiences: 'Due to the recent approaches to the advertisement in virtual space, it seems that choosing and prioritizing pictures should be done based on narration and storytelling, so that [they] engage audiences' (6). As mentioned before, there is no definite method for attracting and engaging the audience; nevertheless, what was frequently specified in the interviews is proportionality, which is pertinent to influencers' creativity.

Narrative advertising

The meaning of narration is storytelling and arranging related and serial events in order to effectively promote the product, service and especially the tourist destination. It is presented in a way that fits with the audience's lifestyle. 'Sometimes I would like to see the advertisement in the context of his/her lifestyle because I can relate to it better' (Belias *et al.*, 2017). On the other hand, regarding how narrative it is, another interviewee's opinion was as follows: 'An influencer can enhance his/her power of narration by merging some story and pictures' (2). One of the interviewees referred to his favourite influencer's method: '... for example, my influencer; he is a writer and writes travelogue. Wherever he goes, he starts narrating from the beginning to the end of his journey. He tells stories and gives me a sense of companionship' (5). In this sense, to be successful, an influencer needs to apply more narrative rather than static methods in order to market a given product or destination.

Destination Promotion

Introducing and promoting the destination is a concern that motivates experts to adopt an influencer's marketing approach. *Destination promotion* has been identified as a main theme based on two codes which have been presented in Table 3.4 as *type of destination* and *introducing*.

Type of destination

Identifying destination type and understanding its real nature is critical to better introduce and promote it, as well as to provide audiences with a better understanding of what is assumed to be

Table 3.4. Destination promotion and related codes.

Theme	Codes	Frequency
Destination promotion	Type of destination	11
	Introducing	25

Source: Author's own work.

advertised. Different types of tourist destinations can be determined based on various criteria such as geographic location, tourism attractions, tourists' activities or destination life cycle. As one of the interviewees argued: 'Destination life cycle is important. For example, in a very initial stage, a micro-influencer seems a good option to promote. But when a destination is placed at growth or maturity stage, a macro-influencer would be more effective' (Belias *et al.*, 2017). Regardless of this argument about which influencer is appropriate at each stage of the destination life cycle, considering this criterion is significant in its nature. Generally, the type of destination must be obvious to both audiences and influencers.

Introducing

The step after recognizing the type of destination is presentation and introduction. Before advertising, it is important to first identify and introduce the destination. A number of interviewees considered one of the appropriate methods to introduce a destination as presence in the place and expression of different dimensions by critically reviewing its strengths and weaknesses. By giving the example of a hotel, one of the interviewees suggested: 'Imagine an influencer who, for example, introduces a hotel. So, intentionally goes and stays there in order to introduce it well. And to show others that how is day and night there, how are the staff who serve there' (2).

Prerequisites for Tourism Businesses

Before selecting an influencer according to the predetermined priorities and criteria to introduce and market their businesses in destination tourism, activists must contemplate a number of things in order to receive the appropriate output from their marketing. In this study, *prerequisites for tourism businesses* have been extracted as a main theme based on four codes including *self-recognition, audience recognition, sale objectives* and *to provide facilities* (Table 3.5).

Self-recognition

To market and introduce a destination, a question must first be answered: Who are we?

Table 3.5. Prerequisites for tourism businesses and related codes.

Theme	Codes	Frequency
Prerequisites for tourism businesses	Self-recognition	10
	Audience recognition	23
	Sale objectives	20
	To provide facilities	6

Source: Author's own work.

Tourism enterprises in each field must be able to achieve a proper and comprehensive knowledge of themselves. One of the interviewees put it this way: 'It [what we are] is related to the nature of the brand and the essence of the brand mission, which is different for each organization. For example, for a five-star hotel, you have to specify your hotel, for example a resort, a hotel boutique or so on' (1). After answering this question, one is able to get closer to the given marketing goals.

Audience recognition

In almost all interviews, the phrase *audience recognition* was frequently mentioned, since in addition to recognizing type of destination and self-knowledge, the audience must be also well monitored, specifically in terms of marketing for a tourist destination. According to one of the interviewees, the importance and definition of audience recognition is as follows: 'When you do not know the audience, the wrong choice of the influencer will lead to losing. That's why knowing audiences is so important and always a priority in digital marketing' (4).

Sometimes it is better to know the customer before selecting an influencer. What some businesses consider in their selection is just the number of followers. As interviewees have stated, one of the most common mistakes is a lack of proper understanding of the market environment. An example in the field of hospitality in one of the interviewee's words is as follows: 'Sometimes for a hotel just being seen is important. The situation of hotels is very complicated. Hotel occupancy rates have been very low during the corona pandemic, especially in cities, where many are going bankrupt. They should work at any cost... however, we must first know who our stakeholders are. It is definitely more important for hotels to recognize the type of followers that the influencer has, and in the next step [influencers] can create a considerable demand' (3). Recognizing the audience is very significant, as an influencer attracts the audience based on his/her viewpoint, which, if it is not in line with the goals of businesses and destination activists, might negatively affect the marketing and branding process.

Sale objectives

The objectives of sales are determined by answering the question What do we want? As one of the interviewees active in the field of food and beverages stated: 'Sometimes sales volume is preferred for me in my restaurant, then I use macro-influencers... but some other times, I may prefer a micro-influencer who visits my restaurant and shares his/her experience with the audiences gradually' (1). In this regard, one of the interviewees gives a good example: 'Introducing a brand of camping equipment on the page of eco-lodges would be more effective than on the page of luxury hotels; even if the eco-lodges page has a smaller number of audiences' (5). Such examples emphasize the importance of recognizing sales objectives, which leads to better targeting of both audiences and advertising channels.

To provide facilities

After selecting an influencer, tourism businesses should consider providing him/her with the required facilities. As one interviewee mentioned: 'Provision of appropriate information to them [influencers] and informing them of the ultimate goal are very important' (6). It also brings about more motivation for influencers in engaging audiences and improving the quality

Table 3.6. Influencer–business interactions and related codes.

Theme	Codes	Frequency
Influencer–business interactions	Adopting a marketing method	7
	Using expert consultants	5
	The importance of concluding a contract	9
	Dispute resolution	9

Source: Author's own work.

of marketing for a business. However, this might not necessarily work in all cases, and it largely depends on the characteristics of the influencer. 'I talked to some influencers several times and I tried to convince them, but finally they did arbitrarily' (3). It therefore demonstrates the importance of selecting a proper influencer.

Influencer–business Interactions

After selecting the proper influencer and recognizing the existing prerequisites, it is time to think about effective interactions with the influencer. Analysing the content of the interviews revealed four relevant codes based on which *influencer–business* interaction theme was extracted (Table 3.6).

Adopting a marketing method

Businesses or investors, together with influencers, draw up their own advertising scenario and agree on how to implement it. In general, each influencer has his/her own way of marketing; however, as two interviewees who are influencers suggested, some methods are general and common among influencers; for instance, holding contests and giving prizes to the followers, setting discounts etc. Such efforts make the audiences feel valued and thus support the influencer, which would result in more effective marketing. It is worthy to note that this only happens if the influencer has sufficient credibility and popularity.

Using expert consultants

One of the most important issues in the relationship and cooperation between influencers and investors is the existence of intermediaries through which messages can be conveyed in an easier way. The use of expert consultants in this field is useful for both investors and influencers. A tourism business or investor, for instance, may not be familiar with all aspects of cyberspace and content production; therefore, existence of a consultant who is professional in this field would clear up many misunderstandings. As one interviewee argued: 'To avoid controversy, first of all, consultants who are expert in the digital marketing field should take on this mission. It is very effective. The first thing they need to do is to reach an agreement with the influencer marketing coordinators' (4). Another interviewee raised immediate problems and suggested: 'In such cases, there should be always a person who is aware of the organization to observe and analyse situations in order to avoid negative propaganda and to keep the audience on track'(1).

The importance of concluding a contract

Concluding a contract is one of the ways to prevent disputes and improve the relationship between investor and influencer, which can, to a large extent, pave the way for communication. Interviewees emphasized the benefits of concluding the contracts. For instance: 'An important challenge is the contract and its depth. I think it can stop future problems. It should not be just oral, but a written conclusion between the two parties and everything should go according to it. Because, for example, as an influencer, I review expectations when I sign a contract, and this signature is always a threat and a pressure factor from investor to me and *vice versa*. Its absence causes problems' (4). Nonetheless, it was considered useless by another interviewee who is a hotel influencer: 'I think, in practice, concluding a contract is not very useful and it is more a symbolic action' (5). Regarding what should be negotiated before contract, one interviewee stated: 'First, a meeting should be arranged in which I (as an investor) specify what I really want, what I am, and how you can have provided me with what I expect. For example, maybe the investor says "I am who I am", or the influencer says "I just work like this". I think both sides should be flexible to reach a common scenario' (4).

Dispute resolution

As mentioned, there will be disputes in any communication. There are a number of disputes, which interviewees have pointed out: 'If investors feel they are being abused, for example, the influencer does advertise just to make money and does not care about the quality' (2). 'In my opinion, when the content produced by the influencer is not the same as the investor has expected, then a conflict might happen' (8). 'Lack of truthfulness and honesty with the audience, abuse of the audience' (4). 'Probably providing incorrect information in any field' (6). In most of the interviews, failure to consider stakeholders' expectations, lack of honesty and integrity, and a focus on earning money and not the quality of the content have been raised as factors creating disputes. When conflicts appear, the biggest mistake is to intensify them and not accept responsibility

from both parties. To resolve the disputes, interviewees have expressed different opinions; for example, two of the interviewees referred to apology, correction of mistakes and avoidance of possible future mistakes. However, one interviewee was of the opinion that resolving the dispute after its occurrence is difficult or even impossible: 'Unfortunately, nothing can be done. During my activity, I talked to many brands that sometimes paid up to $xx to a blogger, but he/she even left the country. The investors can only disclose, but it doesn't work, especially for popular influencers' (5).

Potential of the Instagram Platform

During the interviews, the capabilities and features of Instagram were repeatedly mentioned. As a result, the potential of the Instagram platform was considered as the main theme with eight codes including content production tools, algorithms, word-of-mouth advertising, view rate, image-centric posts, importance of the text, possibility to be anti-advertising, and selling of dreams on Instagram (Table 3.7).

Content creation

Two methods can be used to share photos and videos on Instagram. The first method is posting, which has been the case since the introduction of Instagram, and the second

Table 3.7. Potential of Instagram and related codes.

Theme	Codes	Frequency
Potential of Instagram	Content creation tools	21
	Instagram algorithm	9
	Word-of-mouth advertising	5
	View rate	6
	Image-centric posts	25
	Importance of the text	20
	Possibility to be anti-advertising	6
	To sell dreams	4

Source: Author's own work.

method is stories, which has been added to the new update of this program since 2017. Interviewees were asked about the effectiveness of each of these methods. Most of the responses imply the effectiveness of stories rather than posts. Interviewees mentioned a variety of reasons, including the fact that the stories are more realistic, narrative, concise and easier for users to access. Some also believe that if the content was only a photo, a story is better than a post: 'Stories! because there is no limit to uploading photos in the story compared to the post, so in addition to the main post, leaving detailed stories and more photos is helpful' (4). 'On personal pages I can say "story", because I see that sometimes a lot of Instagram users do not pull the page down at all, and subconsciously see the top stories until they get bored and then close the page' (5).

Although most interviewees emphasized effectiveness of stories, they argued that selection between story and post depends on the type of pages and the type of content. One influencer, for instance, stated: 'In non-personal pages, due to the large number of visitors, posts are seen more' (5). Another influencer argued in this regard: 'Which one is better depends on the page; for example, "trip and joy" uses the post for their tours in order to draw its audiences' attention from the story to the post. This goes back to our marketing funnel. And what should we accustom our audience to?' (4). In addition, three of the interviewees considered the new style of posting called *nano-content* posts, meaning posts with titles and categorized content, to be very effective in the last few years. One interviewee said about these posts: 'Such posts are both more stored and shared, as well as encouraging the audience to open the post when entering "Explore"' (4). On the other hand, one of the interviewees considered the post to be more effective for a number of reasons: 'To me, a post is more important because the story is a temporary thing and you cannot save it for yourself, but you can view the post at any time later' (2). In a similar vein, another interviewee referred to the importance of posts in the ability to leave comments: 'Posts are more preferred because they always remain on the page and there is the ability to leave comments below them' (8).

Instagram algorithm

Each of the programs and social networks has an algorithm and capabilities that must be considered when applying them; otherwise, shared content may be wasted. As one of the interviewees stated, the Instagram algorithm has a substantial impact on the amount of content seen: 'Instagram algorithm is such that if you don't like someone too much, his/her posts and stories will be hidden for you' (1). Another interviewee considered the role and importance of the Instagram algorithm in the number of followers: 'I think the Instagram algorithm has made the number of followers the first important thing for users' (8). Moreover, there are additional features such as report and blocking, posting comments, tags, mentions, and seeing posts in Instagram Explore. A number of interviewees commented on the significance of opinions in the amount of feedback: 'A comment is very important, not every comment, I mean a comment that receives and stimulates others' opinions' (1).

It must be noted that Instagram made the latest changes to its algorithm in 2022. The fields for which changes have been made can be categorized into three groups: Feed and Stories, Explore and Reels. The 2022 Instagram algorithm for Feed and Stories provides users with the ability to sort through the content of the accounts they follow and predicts how likely they are to interact with a post. Such prediction is based on criteria such as information about the post, information about the person who posted, and users' history of interaction with them and their activity across the platform. Regarding the Explore tab, the 2022 algorithm searches previous posts a user has liked or interacted with in order to pull them in a collection of photos and videos from other relevant accounts which have not yet been followed by the user. The purpose is to rank collected photos and videos based on what the algorithm recognizes the user will be most interested in. Finally, the 2022 Instagram algorithm for Reels targets accounts a user follows and accounts he/she does not follow in order to provide him/her with content that the algorithm predicts he/she will always prefer to see[1].

Word-of-mouth advertising

One of the characteristics of social networks is their power in word-of-mouth advertising, which results in people trusting each other. This word-of-mouth communication on the Instagram platform is growing. Interviewees directly and indirectly mentioned this feature of Instagram regarding influencer marketing: 'Due to the word-of-mouth advertising that we are witnessing on Instagram, influencers can play a key role in branding' (5). 'The advertisement that is done is all word-of-mouth. It's all about your trust and belief in the other person' (1). 'The next important point is e-word-of-mouth. For example, I am a fan of someone, and I like what he/she posted, then I re-shared that post' (3).

View rate

The number of posts seen on Instagram pages largely depends on the number of followers. Content on pages with a large following, particularly if they are not fake, has more chance of being seen. Many influencers are trying to be seen in this network because they can increase their effectiveness and efficiency in this way. 'I know a hotel that chooses any influencer, even with only 20,000 followers, for example; because just being seen is important' (3). 'Of course, for them, being seen more, even by a general audience, is more important than being seen less, but through a specific audience' (5). Disregarding the degree of visibility, another interviewee who is a restaurant front-of-house manger believed: 'Now it is only important to be seen; how influential it is [is] not important to us at all' (1). All in all, visibility is one of the most important marketing features that has been supplied to users by Instagram.

Photo-centric posts

Obviously, Instagram is one of the apps that has the ability to share photos and videos. According to conducted interviews, it was inferred from about 80% of the answers that the photo is more important than the text on Instagram. In this regard, influencers have found their place by sharing high-quality photos. Therefore, to produce better content, they must be familiar with photography and photo and video settings. This is well stated by one of the interviewees: 'The higher the quality and more detailed the photos, as well as the better the angle and light of the photos, the more it attracts the audience' (7). Regarding the importance of photos, one of the influencers said: 'The more glamorous the photos are, the more effective they are, because Instagram is photo and video-oriented, and yet the photo has its position' (4).

Another interviewee also emphasized the importance of the photo: 'Photo takes priority, because Instagram is centred on the photo. A person who writes 100 lines, for example, has confused this with the blog' (2). 'Instagram is a visual media. Most of the time, no matter what the text is, you just like the text because you know who has shared it. You do not read the text at all because, for example, he/she is your friend' (1). Acknowledging this, another interviewee argued: 'Instagram makes us lazy. The concept of Instagram is mostly photo ... it is more interesting for me to see photos rather than reading a long text' (3). 'I think the photos [are more important]. I think maybe less than 50% of their audience will even take the time to read the text' (8). One interviewee stated his opinion regarding how to set visual content on Instagram: 'Using video art or visual effects is so important... Music can be very influential and it is even important to share historical photos or talk about historical events. These are influential tools that are not available for a tour leader, while an influencer can easily apply them to convey his/her desired content' (7).

Importance of the text

Interviewees were also asked about the importance of the text and the influencers' writing skill along with the importance of the photos. Five of them considered it necessary to write on Instagram: 'Textual content or captions, in my opinion, play an important role. Unfortunately, this is often ignored' (7). Another interviewee argued: 'Although photos are more attractive, the importance of text should be considered. In written content, one can deal in detail with the events that took place during the trip and interesting stories; something that cannot be done in the photos' (8). 'When I see a photo, I tell myself that he/she wanted to say something that left a photo' (2). One interviewee referred to the complementary role of text for photos: 'In my opinion, photos need deep text or captions to be more effective, and it definitely works' (6). Another interviewee also mentioned the importance of the text in a different way: 'Some of them mostly prefer written texts and some photos or videos. It is certainly more important for the first group' (9). One interviewee expressed his personal preference: 'I look at the text more than the photo, because I think a photo alone makes no sense' (5). However, he had a more inclusive opinion and continued: 'It depends more on the influencer's method. One prefers to share a photo with a very short caption, and another one prefers to share a photo with a long text. It is different for everyone. One cannot say which is better. But when it comes to travel and tourism, I prefer both a good photo and good text, because audiences like to know about that destination and about the influencer's feeling experiences from there. So both are important in this case.' All in all, if an influencer decides to share text on Instagram, it is better to be brief, inclusive and appealing.

Possibility to be anti-advertising

As well as being a great marketing tool, Instagram can also have a counter-advertising feature. Due to the high speed of information dissemination, this network is sometimes used as an anti-advertising tool, particularly against celebrities and influencers: 'In my personal experience, when I came to my role as an influencer in cyberspace, I realized that from now on, living in cyberspace means walking on the razor's edge. The slightest mistake or misunderstanding in speech and behaviour can change the face of an influencer in a second, so much that even if he/she has been introducing certain places such as restaurants or hotels for years, all constructed images will change in the eyes of the audience' (5). It therefore should be

considered by influencers, as any mistake on their part would cause negative propaganda against them. For example, the use of a notorious influencer can negatively affect marketing: 'I believe the lack of commitment [is one reason], so that a number of people become anti-bloggers and anti-influencers and say that this influencer is not good because they do it and tarnish their reputation. You cannot make a mistake and not be seen' (2).

To sell dreams on Instagram

Another feature of the Instagram app, which is imperceptibly imposed on users, especially by influencers, is dream sales. In this visual media, by sharing beautiful photos and promoting a product, a destination or an experience, the backgrounds of dream formation are created in the minds of users. One interviewee describes the sale of a dream as follows: 'Instagram sells dreams. Some influencers give audiences what they want. As a result, they cannot make a real assessment, because now they see their dreams through that lens. But we must note that he/she is showing the wishes, not his/her real lifestyle' (3). According to one of the influencers: 'Some destinations can only be dreamed of, from visas to Corona and ... to expenses, but regarding more available destinations, there is at least a dream that is more real and achievable for them' (4). In this sense, if destination planners could make the dream more achievable for the potential tourists, their chances of successful marketing would be greater.

Discussion and Conclusion

The internet and cyberspace, by filling the gaps and enlarging the circle of individuals' communication, make it possible for ordinary people to be introduced and made famous with the difference that their scope of work is defined in the context of cyberspace. Unlike celebrities and athletes, these individuals, due to having lifestyles and specializations similar to ordinary people in society, have been successful in gaining popularity and trust among different social classes. As a result of this trust, influencer marketing has been created, strengthened and has become one of the sub-branches of the marketing industry. An important issue to note is the impact and role of word-of-mouth e-marketing of influencers who have a large number of followers in cyberspace. This is in line with the findings of Femenia-Serra and Gretzel (2020). The results of their research also show the bright future of influencer marketing, which is shaped by a proper adverti sing campaign.

This paper contributes to the existing literature by identifying that critical attributes must be taken into account when getting influencers to promote tourism destinations. Regarding the characteristics of influencers to be selected by investors, the greatest emphasis of the respondents was on recognizing the purpose of the sale and identifying the right audience. Selecting an influencer based on the features that are important to the investors is primarily related to the purpose of their marketing, as well as the type of destination. For example, to market a luxury destination, selecting a nature-based tourism or ecotourism influencer would not be the best option. Therefore, the genre of the influencer should be determined in this regard. The other factor which is worth considering is the number of followers, which has also been emphasized by De Veirman et al. (2017). They found that Instagram influencers with large numbers of followers are more likeable due to being more popular. However, sometimes it is not easy to recognize if the number of followers is real or fake. On some occasions, influencers with lower numbers of followers would have a greater impact on audiences. As a result, it is important to have constant and effective interaction and public relations with audiences. The issue of gender has also been raised. Although it is wrong to have a gender perspective and the main criterion must be having sufficient ability and expertise, what can be seen from the observations is that females are more prominent in the field of influencer marketing in tourism than males, indicating the greater influence of females. What can be seen is the greater power of females in making content more attractive for their followers. Moreover, investors seem to prefer females to advertise those tourism products and services which are associated with more emotional aspects. However, these claims needs to be investigated further and in more specific studies.

The other feature that greatly changes the popularity of an influencer in cyberspace is responsiveness and availability, since in this space, the person must be responsible for the content he/she has published and answer questions about shared content as much as possible. This is very important for tourists who are planning to travel to a destination, as they usually select and follow people who interact regularly. Another issue to be considered is importance of captions. Since Instagram is an image-driven platform, people might simply see the photos and videos, regardless of the text of the posts. However, findings from analysing interviewees' opinions revealed that people mostly follow those influencers with better content, including both photos/videos and text. Dissemination of up-to-date and accurate information is another factor influencing followers. By ignoring such critical factors, an influencer will lose his/her popularity and, as a result, will be eliminated by competitors.

With regard to the selection of influencer, the question is whether to choose a relevant and specialized influencer or a general interest but more famous one. What makes the selection somewhat easier is understanding the purpose of the marketing. When only sales take precedence, the more famous influencer takes the lead, and when it is important to introduce and present the various dimensions of a destination in a professional way, the more specialized influencer will be the better choice.

The next issue is appropriate methods of marketing through influencers. Narrative and story marketing that is done live has recently become popular and is more effective than banner advertising. Target stakeholders usually prefer this type of marketing as it evokes a sense of experience in the minds of the followers and greatly reduces the commercial aspects of marketing in the eyes of the audience who are tired of advertising.

Empirical results of the present study have major practical implications for destination marketers, as well as tourism influencers. There are several factors to be considered when using influencers to market a tourist destination. These factors may vary from destination to destination and from influencer to influencer. What investors and marketers in tourism destinations should first consider is understanding their organization (what they are), their marketing goals (what they want), the type of destination and its potential, and identifying their target audiences. Choosing the right influencer will then be possible.

Although the present study contributes valuable findings, it is worth noting some gaps for further study in the future. First, one limitation of the present study was impossibility of more face-to-face interviews as a result of the coronavirus pandemic. Second, this research had a general approach to the factors studied. To further this research and gain more detailed findings about the nature of this type of marketing, researchers are recommended to focus on one specific type of tourism such as cultural tourism, ecotourism, food tourism or health tourism. Moreover, the focus can be on a specific destination from a geographical perspective, as well as studying other social networks such as Facebook, YouTube etc.

Note

[1] https://blog.hootsuite.com/instagram-algorithm/ (accessed 13 December 2022).

References

Belias, D., Velissariou, E., Kyriakou, D., Vasiliadis, L., Sdrolias, L. *et al.* (2017) The use of social media as a tool for acquiring knowledge and collaborative environment in tourism: the case of Greece. *Journal of Tourism Research* 16(1), 106–116.

De Veirman, M., Cauberghe, V. and Hudders, L. (2017) Marketing through Instagram influencers: impact of number of followers and product divergence on brand attitude. *International Journal of Advertising* 36(5), 798–828. DOI: 10.1080/02650487.2017.1348035.

Femenia-Serra, F. and Gretzel, U. (2020) Influencer marketing for tourism destinations: lessons from a mature destination. In: Neidhardt, J. and Wörndl, W. (eds) *Information and Communication Technologies in Tourism 2020*. Springer International Publishing, Switzerland, pp. 65–78.

Freberg, K., Graham, K., McGaughey, K. and Freberg, L.A. (2011) Who are the social media influencers? A study of public perceptions of personality. *Public Relations Review* 37(1), 90–92. DOI: 10.1016/j.pubrev.2010.11.001.

Gretzel, U. (2018) Influencer marketing in travel and tourism. In: Sigala, M. and Gretzel, U. (eds) *Advances in Social Media for Travel, Tourism and Hospitality: New Perspectives, Practice and Cases*. Routledge, New York, pp. 147–156.

Hay, B. (2010) Twitter Twitter – but who is listening? A review of the current and potential use of Twittering as a tourism marketing tool. In: *CAUTHE 2010, 20th International Research Conference: 'Challenge the Limits,'* University of Tasmania, February. Available at: https://core.ac.uk/download/pdf/141195401.pdf

Killian, G. and McManus, K. (2015) A marketing communications approach for the digital era: managerial guidelines for social media integration. *Business Horizons* 58(5), 539–549. DOI: 10.1016/j.bushor.2015.05.006.

Leung, D., Law, R., van Hoof, H. and Buhalis, D. (2013) Social media in tourism and hospitality: a literature review. *Journal of Travel & Tourism Marketing* 30(1–2), 3–22. DOI: 10.1080/10548408.2013.750919.

Lim, Y., Chung, Y. and Weaver, P.A. (2012) The impact of social media on destination branding: consumer-generated videos versus destination marketer-generated videos. *Journal of Vacation Marketing* 18(3), 197–206.

Lincoln, Y.S., Guba, E.G. and Pilotta, J.J. (1985) Naturalistic inquiry. *International Journal of Intercultural Relations* 9(4), 438–439. DOI: 10.1016/0147-1767(85)90062-8.

Stepchenkova, S. and Zhan, F. (2013) Visual destination images of Peru: comparative content analysis of DMO and user-generated photography. *Tourism Management* 36, 590–601. DOI: 10.1016/j.tourman.2012.08.006.

Xu (Rinka), X. and Pratt, S. (2018) Social media influencers as endorsers to promote travel destinations: an application of self-congruence theory to the Chinese Generation Y. *Journal of Travel & Tourism Marketing* 35(7), 958–972. DOI: 10.1080/10548408.2018.1468851.

4 Integration of Robotics Technology and Artificial Intelligence in the Transformation of the Tourism Industry: A Critical Viewpoint

Suneel Kumar[1], Varinder Kumar[2] and Kamlesh Attri[3]*

[1]*Department of Commerce, Shaheed Bhagat Singh College, University of Delhi, India;* [2]*Faculty of Management Studies, University of Delhi, India;* [3]*Department of Commerce, Shyam Lal College, University of Delhi, India*

Abstract

Purpose: The present paper aims to highlight technological advancement in the tourism and hospitality sector. This article emphasizes the impact of developing technologies such as robotics technologies and artificial intelligence (AI) on the tourism and hospitality industries. The diverse advanced technologies are combined to boost service and customers' experience in the tourism and hospitality sectors. The study focuses on anticipated challenges and the future scope of AI in the tourism and hospitality sector.

Design/methodology/approach: The literature has been reviewed to acquire information on the role of advanced robotics technologies and artificial intelligence in the tourism and hospitality sector. As a result, a systematic analysis is offered in the form of a viewpoint of AI and robotics in the sectors. The research articles were taken from journals published in Scopus and Research Scholar, from online blogs, from Web of Science (WoS) or from the Australian Business Deans Council (ABDC)/UGC-CARE (Universities Grants Commission-Consortium for Academic and Research Ethics) list. As a result, a systematic analysis is offered in the form of a viewpoint of AI and robotics in the tourism and hospitality sector.

Findings: AI improves experiential tourism services, but it cannot go beyond the human aspect, which is a fundamental factor of experience tourism. AI serves to complement the future of the tourism and hospitality sector in practice. With artificial intelligence of travel, it is easier to schedule the trip, delivering automated, personalized and informative travel services. AI gives travellers a chance, and allows explorers the opportunity, to find out about their propensities, predisposition interests and customized experience. It is not the case nowadays that a travel agent will discuss with them, see them personally and make lengthy telephone conversations to enquire about travel arrangements.

Practical implications: The technological advancement in this sector will have practical implications, especially in tourism marketing, and cause positive and enhanced changes, which will improve the entire experience of the tourist through the use of robotics technology and AI. In travel, tourism and hospitality businesses, new technologies, such as chatbots, virtual reality, language translators and so on may be adopted efficiently.

Originality/value: The current viewpoint examines the role and application of robotics technology and AI with the assistance of appropriate industry hypotheses, theories and models. Therefore, the present study will feature the various technologies currently used and that will be utilized in the future.

*Corresponding author: kamlesh_atri81@yahoo.co.in

© CAB International 2023. *Technology and Social Transformations in Hospitality, Tourism and Gastronomy: South Asia Perspectives* (eds S. Sharma and S. Bhartiya)
DOI: 10.1079/9781800621244.0004

Introduction, Background, Rationale and Literature Review

Robotics advancements and AI technology are among the most inventive innovations in technology-driven times, changing many sectors worldwide. AI was developed as an advanced computer science idea and is now being applied in several lifestyles (Zghyer *et al.*, 2021). Providing alternative perspectives on complicated problems has attracted academic interest. The advancement of electronic systems that can execute functions and activities requiring human intellect can be referred to as AI (Poquet and Laat, 2021). AI is the next step of the tourism market, considering developments in ICT (Zaragoza-Sáez *et al.*, 2021). The intelligent computing skills of AI are well known since they can handle complicated interactions and issues between ideas and operate with a large amount of data (Kirtil and Aşkun, 2021). Moreover, several AI triumphs have followed over the years in systematic searches, identification of characteristics, chatbots, facial recognition, machine language processing and mobile robots (Jia and Zhang, 2021). The epidemic of COVID-19 is having a detrimental effect on the tourism and hospitality sector (Kaushal and Srivastava, 2021). Service robots can be a helpful instrument to establish a high level of physical social distance as individuals seek to avoid physical interaction (Seyitoğlu and Ivanov, 2021). As one method to provide physical distance between tourists and staff, tourism and hospitality firms can thus invest in robotics technology. For example, cleaning robots may be used to regularly clean the common areas of resorts, hotels, airports or other facilities; room service robots can serve meals to visitors' rooms and avoid many guests gathering in hotel restaurants (Seyitoğlu and Ivanov, 2021). Businesses must however consider legal constraints and hygiene standards and carry out a comprehensive cost–benefit analysis on the use of service robots. In the 1980s, significant progress was achieved in the area of technology, and its application was significantly enhanced (Ma *et al.*, 2021). In the 1990s, the technical environment, notably in AI, made tremendous progress (Zhang and Lu, 2021). The rise was mainly due to advanced and new technologies that enabled developers to utilize enormous amounts of data, construct robots and strive towards better

computer capacities (Yu *et al.*, 2021). The AI idea has since gone on a long way and altered technological power. AI has reached its zenith in the 21st century and can significantly influence individuals, companies and industries.

AI technology is employed in a digitized era in several businesses, not simply in the field of information technology. For example, autonomous vehicles, robotic nurses, airports, Google Maps, chatbots, human vs. machine games and several more sectors can make use of AI (Rust and Huang, 2021). The worldwide software market for AI is expected to expand quickly in future years to about USD 126 billion by 2025 (Liu, 2020). There are various applications in the entire AI sector, including natural language processing, robotic processing, automation and machine learning. Secondly, in 2020, the market for robots was estimated at USD 23.67 billion (Mordor Intelligence, 2021). By 2026, it is anticipated to reach USD 74 billion and have a CAGR (compound annual growth rate) of 20.4% during the projection period 2021–2026 (Mordor Intelligence, 2021). Robotics technology and AI are present in some of the most important industries, such as healthcare (Vijai and Wisetsri, 2021), retail and e-commerce (Kalia, 2021), manufacturing, automotive, logistics, transport, financial services and banking, life sciences, insurance, telecommunications, energy (Berdiyorova *et al.*, 2021), tourist travel and hospitality (Li *et al.*, 2021), and media (Hassan, 2021). The footprint of AI is expanding rapidly every day in more sectors throughout the world. AI technology's popularity and use are growing in the industry by boosting innovation and minimizing human procedures and activities (Wu *et al.*, 2021). AI is utilized by numerous sectors in various tasks such as sales and marketing, customer service, finance and banking.

The epidemic of COVID-19 significantly impacted the tourism and hospitality market in 2020 as countries implemented worldwide travel restrictions, which restricted the need for services supplied by these facilities (Gautam, 2021). However, the hotel and other travel accommodation industries are projected to recover from the shock as its occurrence is a 'black swan', i.e. it is not linked to continuing or fundamental market or global economic problems (Patil and Kolhe, 2021). Furthermore, increased usage of social media and mass media access have a beneficial effect on tourism and the hotel sector (Pop *et al.*, 2021). Travellers become aware of tourist sites and experiences worldwide by sharing their travel information, photos and videos on social media platforms (Wendemagegnehu, 2021). As a result, the world hotel and other tourism lodging industries were predicted to increase, at a CAGR of 19.1%, or by USD 673.02 trillion in 2020 to USD 801.9 billion in 2021 (Research and Markets, 2021). The COVID-19 impact and recovery offers important information on the worldwide hotel and other tourism accommodations business as it emerges from the COVID-19 shutdown to assist strategists, marketers and senior management with the essential information they need. The rise is mainly due to the rearrangement of business and the recovery from the impact of COVID-19, which led previously to tight confinement measures comprising social and physical distancing and remote operations and the closure of commercial activities, which resulted in operational problems. As a result, the market is forecast, with CAGRs of 7% in 2025, to reach USD 1052.84 billion with 37% of the world's market. In 2020, Asia Pacific was the world's largest region in the hotel and other travel accommodation sector (Research and Markets, 2021). North America represented 27% of the worldwide hotel market and another travel market, the second biggest region. In the global hotel and tourism market, Africa was the smallest region (Research and Markets, 2021). Resorts and hotels use technology that changes the experiences of customers. Some technologies contribute to significant improvements and savings in the hotel and other tourism markets. In the tourism and hospitality sector, the most critical developments are near-field communication (NFC), AI technology and robotics (Research and Markets, 2021). This viewpoint illustrates how robotics and technology for AI have infiltrated the tourism environment and produced revolutionary changes in the industrial environment. Furthermore, this viewpoint provides a critical understanding of the different AI technologies used, their consequences, problems, and future possibilities for travel, tourism and hospitality. It might also highlight the potential of AI and its consequences for the industrial environment in technology-driven times. A thorough evaluation has been conducted to understand how AI turns ordinary tourism into an intelligent industrial hub.

Specific Objectives of the Study

The objective of this paper is to highlight technological advancement in the tourism and hospitality sector. The diverse advanced technologies are combined to boost service and customer experience in the sector. It seeks to address the following objectives.

I.   to study the impact of developing technologies such as robotics technologies and AI in the tourism and hospitality industry;

II. to examine the anticipated challenges and future applications of AI in the sector.

Research Methodology

For the study, data have been collected from a secondary source. The literature has been reviewed to acquire information on the role of advanced robotics technologies and AI in the tourism and hospitality sector. As a result, a systematic analysis is offered in the form of a viewpoint of AI and robotics in the sector. The research articles were taken from journals published in Scopus and Research Scholar, from online blogs, from Web of Science (WoS) or from the Australian Business Deans Council (ABDC)/ UGC-CARE (Universities Grants Commission-Consortium for Academic and Research Ethics) list. After critical examination of the collected literature, the scope, impact, challenges and future applications of AI in the tourism and hospitality sectors were discussed in detail.

Discussion: Integration of Robotics Technology and AI in the Tourism Sector

With progression in computer technology, robotics and AI are becoming more trustworthy and their position is improving in the corporate sector. Indeed, AI is rapidly being used by the tourism and hospitality sectors to perform customer care activities, mainly in hotels and resorts. Therefore, the researchers addressed this essay's integration of robotics and how AI is revolutionizing the tourism and hospitality sector. The discussion is divided into four sections. The first section discusses the scope of AI in the tourism sector. The second section is mostly focused on the impact of AI on the industry, within which applications such as virtual tourism, chatbots, virtual assistance, autonomous vehicles, Google Maps, language translation services, robotics and facial recognition services are discussed. The third section describes the anticipated challenges and problems of AI in the tourism and hospitality sectors. The fourth section discusses future applications of AI.

Scope of AI in the tourism sector

The term AI was coined by John McCarthy in 1956 as: '...the capacity of external data to be correctly interpreted and learn from these data and utilise them to reach particular objectives and tasks via flexible adaptation'. There are a few intriguing findings in the travel, tourism and hospitality industries that cause AI to be used. There has recently been very little use of AI by firms such as Google Travel, Tata Consultancy and Tripadvisor. This paper has revealed the following significant discoveries that benefit companies:

- A Tata Consultancy Services (TCS) study found that 85% of travel and hospitality services suppliers employ AI. Studies show that this might be because innovative digital sales increased rapidly and were anticipated to reach USD 800 billion by 2020 (Samala *et al.*, 2020).
- 74% of tourists plan on the internet, and more than 45% use smartphones to plan their holidays, according to a survey by Google and Tripadvisor Travel (Peranzo, 2019).
- Another poll found that almost 85% of leisure tourists only decide on activities and their plans once they arrive (Google, 2016). In addition, more than 36% of consumers are prepared to pay more if the booking experience is interactive and straightforward. Nearly 80% of customers choose self-service to discover their information

(Peranzo, 2019) and around 90% expect helpful information on their journey to the destination (Google, 2016).

In all these outcomes, the trend towards internet and self-service technology seems to be recommended for visitors. These findings would make marketers use AI to provide improved consumer experience in interactive and self-service technology. The polls reveal the technological trend of customers and the element of 'timeliness'. The services they obtain are very timely for consumers. Most visitors are not ready to receive services in advance but expect these services when they travel (Samala *et al.*, 2020). Furthermore, findings show that most customers choose self-service technology over conventional services. By using AI, self-service technologies are substantially achievable.

Moreover, these variables impact travel, tourism and hospitality industries in numerous other aspects. The selection of tourism, travelling and hospitality services includes natural resources, general infrastructure, tourist infrastructure and essential aspects (Fernández *et al.*, 2020). Natural resources encompass natural beauty, lakes, hills, grasslands, mountains, flora and wildlife, and meteorological conditions like regional temperature, snowfall and humidity. Basic facilities include highways and public and private transportation. Tourist infrastructure comprises hotels, restaurants, cafés, nightclubs, amusement parks, sports and entertainment activities, water parks, zoos, theatres, trekking, outdoor adventures and retail malls (Ameri, 2021). Finally, infrastructure for destination tourism comprises human resources and security measures. A vast range of information may be generated by AI on all essential aspects, such as natural resources, basic infrastructure, tourist infrastructure and destination tourist infrastructure (Gretzel *et al.*, 2015). IT technology may surpass human performance by delivering a wide range of information in no time on the most critical aspects (Grace *et al.*, 2018). AI can, under some conditions, exceed human service. AI readily meets consumer expectations by providing timely information on essential variables such as natural resources, basic infrastructure facilities, tourist infrastructure facilities and destination attractiveness infrastructure (Dwyer *et al.*, 2008). This information can be found in

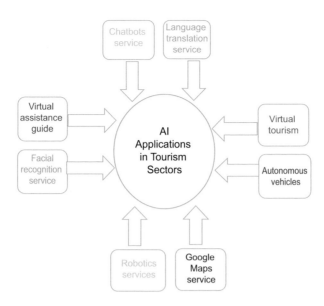

Fig. 4.1. AI applications in tourism.
Source: Author's own work.

interactive messaging, self-service technology, virtual tourism through virtual guides, chatbots, multimedia tours, virtual guide interactive maps, interactive booking processes, facial recognition software technologies, translations of languages, cross-selling and upselling, lower prices and simple shopping (Pencarelli, 2020).

Impact of AI in the tourism sector

In the field of AI, numerous new technologies have developed. These technologies have been helpful in providing visitors with new experiences. They include virtual guides, virtual tourism, facial recognition technologies, autonomic vehicles, and applications for virtual reality, chatbots, robots, Google Maps, language translators, audio tours and shopping facilities (Fig. 4.1).

Virtual tourism service

Due to the COVID-19 epidemic, hotels, destinations and passengers have suffered, and the tourism industry has halted. Local holidays frequently become impossible, and corporate travel also diminished, given that more people work from home (Karim *et al.*, 2020). Creating marketing and new virtual AI services can,

nonetheless, make a significant impact in future years. Virtual tourism and journeys are starting, and hotels and locations that recognize the trend are becoming successful as the world gets back to normal and visitors pack their bags again (Fredericks, 2021). Virtual tourism offers consumers an authentic experience, via the use of technology, of activities and locations. There are many kinds of virtual tourism services. However, generally, there is a combination of virtual reality, still pictures, audio interaction, video and other electronic forms that allow users to gain a unique experience through photographs or the internet and websites (Fredericks, 2021). For a 3D experience, viewers may access virtual tourism content via a VR (virtual reality) headset, but they can also see content on a standard computer or mobile system. Because people may enjoy the activities from the comfort of their home, virtual tourism offers several apparent advantages:

- Tourists will experience locations without travelling, which means they are not restricted to available airlines, or subjected to travel and security difficulties. Moreover, they do not need to consider climatic conditions or time frames (Fredericks, 2021).

- Virtual tourism technology provides excellent marketing potential. In place of the flat photos in a brochure or on a website, prospective visitors may get a 360 degree perspective of a property and its facilities. In this manner, a facility will improve its chances for viewers to visit and enable them to share the virtual services with loved ones (Fredericks, 2021).

Virtual assistance service

A virtual tour assistant is an expert who can support the customer from across the world, and as in other sectors today, the travel and hospitality industries are affected by AI, machine learning and extensive data analysis to a modest extent. Virtual assistants are becoming one of the main pillars of guaranteeing excellent, and personally tailored customer experiences for most marketing companies. Therefore, Gartner anticipates that around 15% of business will be enacted by 2021 using virtual assistants (Priyadarshini, 2020). Business equipment that does not leverage new technologies will slip behind more creative businesses. A virtual personal assistant is one way a travel and hospitality business may contribute to a pleasant client experience. Virtual assistants make accessing hotel bookings and reservations easy. Apple's Siri has been in existence since 2011 and is a clever piece of computer software, which is also a personal assistant (Trends, 2020).

The rise of virtual online aids changes guests' ways of buying and consuming services. With a sleek, conversational virtual assistant that improves sales productivity and customer satisfaction, Hyatt, one of the globe's biggest brands in tourism and hospitality today, saves as much as USD 4.4 million annually (Trends, 2020). Hyatt has provided its clients with cost-saving, time-saving and income service options by automating and simplifying regular operations for travellers on the move. There are thus the following areas where businesses and consumers benefit from virtual assistant services, travel and hospitality:

- **Reservations and bookings**: Hoteliers and hotel staff at the front desk deal with regular, repeated enquiries daily. Basic questions are addressed: Are there any rooms available for tomorrow? What are your room rates? Is your hotel providing conference facilities? In order to deal with most of the daily repeated queries, essential work and other administrative tasks encountered by travel and hospitality officials, virtual assistance can be arranged.
- **Dining recommendations and orders**: Visitors may, from the comfort of their hotel room, enquire about dining options. They may also place their order for dinner. There is no need to contact the front desk.
- **Concierge services**: To provide simplified concierge services for the visitor, virtual assistants may engage with them. For example, virtual assistants may provide individual local advice, manage and check out customers' registrations, provide information on features in different guest rooms, organize tours and supply customers with answers to other basic requests. With the aid of a virtual assistant, visitors may also enquire about fees, ask for addresses and check or cancel bookings on the move without contacting a human operator.

Google Maps service

Google Maps allows tourists to navigate a new place, find the quickest and simplest routes, and is the go-to digital map. However, it works like a travel planner since people can rapidly look for sites to stay, visit, dine and do activities (Steeves, 2019). In Google Maps, AI technology has enhanced information by informing travellers of accidents, road construction, strikes and heavy traffic. Now that Google has joined the sector for tourist attractions, businesses may start collecting and accepting payments and reservations through Reserve with Google, Google Maps, Google Search and Google Voice Search. Recently, Google has launched a revamp of Google Travel, one of the finest web pages, which will replace Google Trips (Steeves, 2019). At this stage, the visitor may get information on the trip, modify flight details and hotel bookings and examine the places bookmarked.

Chatbots service

Chatbots in tourism are one of the world's most active customer-facing business innovations and provide tremendous travel and tourism opportunities. The chatbot is now a credo in many sectors, and the tourism industry is no exception (Nair, 2019). The technology transformation has significantly shaken the tourism business for well over a decade. This is testament to digital travel agents, flight ticket reservations through an online app, and web checks. Travel chatbots are being widely used as the most outstanding example of this constant change. There is plenty to make life simpler for consumers and providers of travel services alike using AI-powered chatbots. Conversational AI in the tourism industry pays enormous returns. Studies have revealed that more than 55% of Millennials are likely to perceive chatbots favourably (Nair, 2019). It is projected that Millennials spend around USD 200 billion. Travellers would thus be urged to make use of any technology that enhances their experience. Conversational AI can change the travel sector for the better in the following main areas:

- **Saving time and trouble**: Regular enquiries and FAQs are the major requests handled by travel agents or hotel employees. It is very inefficient for human customer care service agents to address these issues frequently. When a company has enough options within the conversational AI arena, these regular enquiries may be resolved by chatbots easily (McGloin, 2020). This allows staff to solve complicated client issues and take care of other management responsibilities that need human interaction. The ability of chatbots to reply to common questions may be a significant motivating element for staff, who are thus relieved of a monotonous job. This increases their efficiency and performance.

- **Customer commitment and customization**: Chatbots are online to handle simple consumer concerns 24/7, 365 days a year. This continuous reliability improves the customer experience in all industries. However, it is especially beneficial for customers in the tourism and hospitality sector, as they can promptly fix their concerns travelling between time zones.

- **A rich source of data and information**: The client has the ability to retrieve data on a conversational AI platform quickly. Chatbots are also a rich source of information about consumers, providing an overview of their buying history, attitudes, experience, tests, positive and negative comments and feedback. Players in the tourism and travel business may use these data in a variety of ways. They can give tailored guidelines based on the inputs from customers. Based on the information collected, they may customize their marketing messages to individual consumers. Future consumer behaviour and intention are predictable for conversational analyses.

Chatbots can improve consumer experience and increase their commitment to the business. When dealing with regular enquiries, they are considerably more effective than human staff. They are a great source of customer data and continually refresh them. Moreover, from a price and income-generation viewpoint, they are a great asset.

Robotics service

When referring to robots and their function, it is necessary first to determine what they are. A robot is a machine that is created to perform complicated actions or tasks mechanically, and certain robots are intended to look like people. These are termed androids. Many robots assume no such shape. Advanced and modern robots could be automated or semi-autonomous, using AI and language recognition technologies. However, most robots are programmed with high accuracy to execute specific jobs, such as the industrial robot in manufacturing or production processes.

Robots continue to penetrate the tourism and hospitality sector and modernize it, and through these technological advances, current services and delivery techniques, and thus service management and marketing tactics might alter drastically. Robots are also another form of AI innovation, which enhances its tourism sector footprint. The Internet of Things (IoT) technology is used to perform simple operations like opening windows, turning off the TV, managing systems to guarantee that luggage is efficiently checked in, and welcoming customers at a hotel. The employment of robots can result in speed, economic efficiency and even greater precision. For instance, chatbots allow a hotel or travel firm, even if employees are not accessible, to give 24/7 help via internet chat services or immediate messaging, providing speedy response times. Meanwhile, the whole process may be speeded up by a robot employed during the check-in procedure. The following are real-world examples of hotels that deploy robots in the tourism and hospitality sectors:

- **Staffed hotel**: The Henn-na Hotel, the first hotel globally to be fully equipped with robots, is located in Nagasaki, Japan. Robots are used in the hotel to provide information, reception, parking and check-in and check-out services, and integrating voice and facial recognition technologies (Revfine.com, 2020).
- **Hilton**: Connie is a Hilton-owned robot receptionist. The robot can communicate and answer guests' enquiries due to its speech acknowledgement skills using an AI platform built by IBM. The system also learns and adapts with each contact,

enhancing its responses (Revfine.com, 2020).

Facial recognition service

In tourism and hospitality, facial recognition technologies are also developed and used more frequently. This is particularly important since tourism businesses have to deal with many customers and visitors. Therefore, any technology that may help accelerate procedures is highly advantageous. Furthermore, security and safety are significant issues at hotels, resorts and airports. Facial recognition may be used to identify people more quickly, provide certain persons with access to places and keep others out. Technologies of facial recognition also facilitate the identification and capture of criminals (Revfine.com, 2021). This, in turn, leads to greater security for travellers or visitors to destinations. In addition, customer experience may be improved immediately by the capacity to recognize faces. The following services in the tourism and hospitality sector use facial recognition (Fig. 4.2).

- **Data analysis service**: Data play a vital part in providing exceptional service and optimizing operations for hotels and other

Fig. 4.2. Facial recognition services.

organizations in tourism and hospitality. In this field, facial recognition technology is anticipated to play a more critical role in future years, allowing data to be automatically gathered. The system may also determine who someone is, assess their age, and match them to a picture in a database. This, therefore, may provide reliable data on customers' ethnicity and how they react to various places and services, and companies can use this to identify significant trends.

- **Security service**: Another service is to enhance security. Facial recognition checks a guest's ID and provides them with access to the guest room, the fitness centre or other hotel facilities. Facial recognition can sometimes be employed for crime prevention. Using an internal database, the system may warn hotel employees quickly about persons who have a history of poor behaviour so that they might be removed from the premises or referred to the police.
- **Personalization service**: Another straightforward use of facial recognition is to increase visitor and guest personalization. Tourism and other businesses may rapidly identify and adapt services to customers by comparing faces with those in a database. For example, hotels may ask customers to provide their photo during the booking process. When the hotel camera recognizes you on arrival, staff may greet you with your name and utilize the reservation information to enhance their service. It may also be used to identify customers who have previously visited the hotel and reward them accordingly.
- **Payment service**: Among the most exciting applications of facial recognition is the fast and efficient processing of payments. Mastercard has started to experiment with a 'selfie payment' system, which confirms the payment via a phone camera, with the face linked to one in a computer database.

Language translation service

For many countries, tourism is an economic engine, and its importance is increasing due to globalization. Despite many tourists travelling worldwide, however, there is still one obstacle that might impair their experience: language. AI translation is a technology that tourism may employ to overcome language obstacles and boost the market's potential. There are several forms of AI software that translate, such as Google Translate, Triplingo, sayhi, and Microsoft Translator (Zaino, 2020). It can be difficult to go abroad if communication problems exist. This difficulty can only be overcome if a local guide is used by travellers. Software programs can substitute for a local guide:

- **Google Translate**: This application allows tourists to convert 108 languages and access 59 offline languages. This technology would even enable travellers to talk with local residents. If the traveller chooses the option 'Conversation mode', Google Translate delivers audio voice services. Tourists may use their camera for a quick translation of a menu in 90 languages (Zaino, 2020). Instant language translation in 43 languages is available. Using icons, you may click to draw, take pictures, talk or text. Google Translate is very simple to use.
- **Microsoft Translator**: With Microsoft Translator, text, audio and images from English can be converted into over 60 languages (Zaino, 2020). The app is perfect for travellers and tourists, with a multi-person translation function that allows tourists to link their appliances and communicate in several languages with as many as 100 people. The divided-screen feature allows tourists to view a sentence, while someone across from them may read the translation. Language packs for offline translating are the best feature of this app. Tourists may also learn how to correctly say parts of the sentence they are translating using translation guidelines and pronunciation aids instead of just relying on voices.

Autonomous vehicle service

Autonomous vehicle service may impact all transport-oriented industries, including the tourism and travel sectors. Driverless cars are capable of changing how people actually live, operate and travel in cities. Autonomous vehicles may be the next great industry-wide idea for manufacturing firms, together with Blockchain. Blockchain technology is an enhanced database system that enables the sharing of information in a corporate network in an open and honest manner. Using blockchain technology and smart contracts, it is possible to build a decentralized network for automobile sharing. Transport is a core-level service covering conveying passengers and luggage at airports, car rental, city taxis and touring in vehicles (Bainbridge, 2018). Replacement of these operations with autonomous cars would generate significant upset for long-standing businesses that use human drivers, however these automobiles significantly reduce human error, so the frequency of accidents would be reduced considerably. An increasing number of such cars would also reduce congestion because unacceptable driving behaviour causes traffic jams. Apart from this, autonomous cars could also provide the following potential benefits for tourism and travel sectors:

- **New tourism possibilities**: Travellers can take entirely personal tours on demand. City tours using buses can now be carried out by autonomous cars.
- **Multi-day trips**: A traveller can journey from X to Y to Z on a multi-day schedule. This will be highly competitive with existing multi-day schedule excursions now offered by local travel providers. The hotel agreements to be used for these tours are the OTA agreements and not the local tour operators, which further centralizes the purchasing power of hotels.
- **Changes in hotels**: Hotels can effectively sell independent sightseeing trips from the desk (or its digital substitute) to schedule a route intended for that client. Thus, there is certainly an exciting opportunity for new methods to expand loyalty points and change the way luggage is transported between different hotels.
- **New role for distributors**: Autonomous car tour distributors will have to become custodians. The vehicle will need to know far more information about a client to personalize a tour completely. If distributors do not progress to deal with this, customers will directly arrange autonomous car tours.

The challenges of AI in the tourism sector

Artificial intelligence now has a lot of beneficial impacts on the field of tourism and hospitality. However, some problems and challenges still need to be tackled. So, three major concerns are analysed in detail: issues concerning the acceptance and use of AI by tourists; replacement of humans with robots; and the dilemma of ethics and biases in AI (Bulchand, 2020) (Fig. 4.3).

Issues concerning the acceptance and use of AI by tourists

With AI, the first problem is the concerns, opinions and impressions of travellers. Tourists can be categorized into groups: innovators, early adopters, early majority, later majority, and latecomers, as with any other innovation or invention. Based on the dangers and advantages of AI, three user types have been identified: laggards (who see a high risk and low benefit for AI), enthusiasts (who embrace benefits and consider risk levels low), and rationalists (who see both dangers and advantages of AI) (Bulchand, 2020). As with the use of robots, the significant motivation is that it is seen as beneficial and efficient, as with other innovations. However, AI is a severe issue when there is damage to humanity. The three primary worries of visitors are: fear of monitoring; a division of the population over the use, or not, of AI; and society being entirely technologically driven.

Regarding monitoring, several authors have noted a threat to the confidentiality of AI systems since they collect enormous volumes of data and gain insights. Therefore, there is a possibility that an AI division would occur due to lack of access. Moreover, owing to the sense of danger, certain people may not engage in AI systems. As for the worry about a technology-led society, travellers will undoubtedly have to pick between more robotic, automated, computerized, efficient and cost-effective services and less-automated and human luxury services. The difficulties described above cannot be resolved, but technological developments and human cooperation are needed.

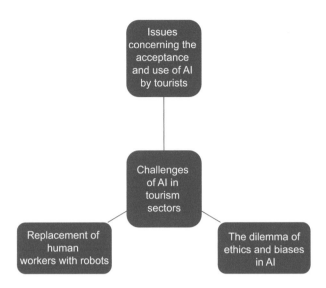

Fig. 4.3. Anticipated challenges of AI in the tourism and hospitality sectors. Source: Author's compilation.

Replacement of humans with robots and AI

Concerns about job losses due to AI were covered by several corporate and academic types of research. According to the World Economic Forum, AI technology is expected to displace over 75 million jobs by 2022 (Pedamkar, 2020). Some figures are even more intimidating. As another piece of McKinsey research states, 30% of the present world employment may be replaced by AI-based robots, while the AI specialist and risk capitalist Kai-Fu Lee hypothesized that within the next 10–15 years, 40% of world employment will be displaced by AI-based bots (Pedamkar, 2020). A new breed of technologies (such as chatbots and robotics) that can now compete with and substitute for humans in practically every activity is emerging with the rise of AI innovations. So that means the tourist industry, which has been insulated from this scenario for a long time, is at risk. Automation may replace around 25% of hospitality employees over the next decade; a radical shift for robotics (Pedamkar, 2020). As a result, traditional tourist operations (like the hotel front counter) may eventually go. AI has been called the biggest threat to human life by some authors. Indeed, displacing employees is one of the major worries about AI in tourism, not only due to job losses but also because of employees' lack of a sense of belonging.

The dilemma of ethics and biases in AI

The influence of AI is equivalent to that of automated equipment such as computers and machines, as part of the fourth Industrial Revolution. This poses some ethical problems to be explored. Some of these, e.g. invasion of privacy and concerns of an entirely technologically driven society, have been suggested. Another significant and severe issue linked to the broad usage of AI is bias (Siau and Wang, 2020). All people are biased, e.g. race, religion, gender and financial status, and that includes those who build AI systems. The concern is that AI is considerably stronger than humans and this might make it easier to amplify bias included in programs (Lloyd, 2018). This may lead to AI learning how to deploy biased structures that then are reproduced. In this respect, AI systems were suggested for transparency, robustness and predictability. AI systems will always need to make balanced choices that maximize the advantages of all players. Finally, the constructed AI systems should incorporate ethics as a basis when robust learning ability systems are designed.

Future applications of AI in the tourism and hospitality sector

In a wave of advancements and applications in the tourism sector, AI plays a vital role and substantially transforms the tourism and service experience. At the beginning of 2020, the global spread of COVID-19 triggered economic decline throughout the world. The broad application of telehealth, UAV monitoring, robotic healthcare and nurses, Siri, and Google Duplex artificial intelligence has not only replaced medical workers in order to perform many high-risk duties but has also been a special human companion in dangerous times (Siteminder, 2020). We saw robots in science fiction movies just 15 years ago, which shook the mind and reached the boundaries of human imagination. Facial technology, fingerprint biometrics, human-speaking computers, and functioning AI looked like worlds away when Tom Cruise and Will Smith appeared in their first action movies. However, there are now several channels and sectors in which AI may be applied to improve services. These are not just in the airport and science fields, but also tourism and hospitality sectors. These might be stunning and unexpected. For example, a whole hotel room may become a popular tourist attraction using AI technologies. After entering the room, guests can choose to turn it into their chosen place. The whole room is turned into a virtual 3D environment similar to the client's preferred location. Then the visitor can enjoy 3D views of his/her favourite place, in the room.

The global positioning system (GPS) will shortly be taken over by the visual positioning system (VPS). VPS allows the location of a particular environment on a map (Samala *et al.*, 2020), and gives a realistic and visual view to the visitor of stores, businesses, resorts, hotels, supermarkets, malls, movie theatres, cafés, places to eat and leisure areas. It utilizes many pictures of the surroundings to create a 3D environment. In addition, arrows will highlight how the user must travel, and a little map will be shown to inform you where to go. In the coming years, we will also witness robotics technology that serves hotel guests, bringing their baggage to the room, serving them meals and snacks, and providing a laundry and housekeeping service (Samala *et al.*, 2020).

Such systems are now in use at a few hotels and resorts.

There could be many more surprising areas lying ahead relating to consumer servicing where AI may be used.

Conclusion

The influence of AI increases every day in the tourism and hospitality sector. With the expanding use of new technologies, unfathomable dimensions are predictedt. It has been predicted that by 2026 the AI tourism and hospitality market will exceed USD 1.2 billion, which is estimated at around 9.7% CAGR over the projection period 2021–2026 (Industryarc, 2021). The majority of hotels and restaurants rely substantially on satisfied customers to create their image, and AI technology can help in many ways, including customization improvement, personalizing suggestions and ensuring rapid response times, even in the absence of employees. The successful performance of the tourism and hospitality sector is one of the major drivers for the projected development. However, creative and new technologies like machine learning and AI will lead to substantial industrial developments. The robot service impresses tourists by delivering surprising offerings, continuously involving tourists, and creating a new and exciting atmosphere for clients. Hotel robots provide support for tourists through delivery to hotel rooms, luggage delivery to the room, housekeeping, and food and snacks. Through its indoor service and the support of hostelling facilities, robotics is continuously improving tourist loyalty and experience. With the number of tourists increasing, it is necessary to separate services providers from customized services while maintaining the needs of tourists. Although AI technology will provide many advantages in business, it could also generate many difficulties and challenges. For example, it would not be simple to integrate various forms of AI in the commercial environment of tourism. Business requires appropriate funds in order to construct a secure and resilient information system. The growth of virtual assistance, facial recognition, chatbots, robots and other AI technology would restrict genuine human connection in the tourism and hospitality industry. This might have a negative impact on the end user. The technology-led strategy may create new, complicated, unknown technological problems. Tourist marketers must integrate technology innovation smoothly to make the use of technology simple and at the same time beneficial to all parties. This procedure can be rather long as the technology of AI is still in the early stages.

Suggestions and Future Scope for Research

The concept of AI is exceptionally fresh and robust. Therefore, research is needed in various fields for AI travel and tourism growth. Three main aspects may be explored in future: the consumer's acceptance of AI travel and tourism sectors; the above impacts of AI on employment and human substitution; and the influence of AI on the tourism and hospitality industry's economy. Rigorous studies on AI in tourism are thus necessary to evaluate the technology's overall implications, which will be helpful to understand both the favourable and unfavourable impacts of AI on the tourism and hospitality industry, its enterprises and its users.

References

Ameri, A. (2021) The effects of physical and non-physical dimensions of place on the formation of place image: the influence of online information on the interpretation of American cities. Dissertation, North Carolina State University.

Bainbridge, A. (2018) Prepare for impact: autonomous vehicles will reshuffle the travel industry. Available at: https://www.phocuswire.com/Autonomous-vehicles-impact-tourism (accessed 21 December 2022).

Berdiyorova, I., Akhtamova, P. and Ganiev, I.M. (2021) Artificial intelligence in various industries. In: *Proceedings of the conference development issues of innovative economy in the agricultural sector*, Tashkent State University of Economics, March 25–26, 2021, pp. 750–757.

Bulchand, G.J. (2020) Impact of artificial intelligence in travel, tourism and hospitality. In: Xiang, Z., Fuchs, M. and Hopken, W. (eds) *Handbook of e-Tourism*. Springer.

Dwyer, L., Edwards, D.C., Mistilis, N., Roman, C., Scott, N. *et al.* (2008) Megatrends underpinning tourism to 2020: analysis of key drivers for change. University of Canberra, Australia.

Fernández, J.A.S., Azevedo, P.S., Martín, J.M.M. and Martín, J.A.R. (2020) Determinants of tourism destination competitiveness in the countries most visited by international tourists: proposal of a synthetic index. *Tourism Management Perspectives* 33, 100582.

Fredericks, L. (2021) The complete guide to virtual tourism in 2021. Available at: https://www.cvent.com /en/blog/hospitality/virtual-tourism (accessed 16 February 2021).

Gautam, P. (2021) The effects and challenges of COVID-19 in the hospitality and tourism sector in India. *Journal of Tourism and Hospitality Education* 11, 43–63. DOI: 10.3126/jthe.v11i0.38242.

Google, T.W. (2016) How mobile influences travel decision making in can't-wait-to-explore moments. Available at: https://www.thinkwithgoogle.com/intl/en-gb/consumer-insights/ consumer-journey/mobile-influence-travel-decision-making-explore-moments/ (accessed 21 December 2022).

Grace, K., Salvatier, J., Dafoe, A., Zhang, B., and Evans, O. (2018) When will AI exceed human performance? Evidence from AI experts. *Journal of Artificial Intelligence Research*, 62, 729–754.

Gretzel, U., Sigala, M., Xiang, Z. and Koo, C. (2015) Smart tourism: foundations and developments. *Electronic Markets* 25(3), 179–188.

Hassan, A. (2021) The usage of artificial intelligence in new media. *European, Asian, Middle Eastern, North African Conference on Management & Information Systems* 229–240.

Industryarc (2021) Travel & hospitality AI market – forecast (2021 - 2026). Available at: https://www.indust ryarc.com/Report/18662/travel-hospitality-ai-market.html (accessed 21 December 2022).

Jia, K. and Zhang, N. (2021) Categorization and eccentricity of AI risks: a comparative study of the global AI guidelines. *Electronic Markets* 1–13.

Kalia, P. (2021) Artificial intelligence in e-commerce: a business process analysis. In: *Artificial Intelligence*. CRC Press. DOI: 10.1201/9781003095910.

Karim, W., Haque, A., Anis, Z. and Ulfy, M.A. (2020) The movement control order (mco) for COVID-19 crisis and its impact on tourism and hospitality sector in Malaysia. *International Tourism and Hospitality Journal* 3(2), 1–7.

Kaushal, V. and Srivastava, S. (2021) Hospitality and tourism industry amid COVID-19 pandemic: perspectives on challenges and learnings from India. *International Journal of Hospitality Management* 92, 102707. DOI: 10.1016/j.ijhm.2020.102707.

Kirtil, İ.G. and Aşkun, V. (2021) Artificial intelligence in tourism: a review and bibliometrics research. *Advances in Hospitality and Tourism Research (AHTR)* 9, 205–233. DOI: 10.30519/ahtr.801690.

Li, M., Yin, D., Qiu, H. and Bai, B. (2021) A systematic review of AI technology-based service encounters: Implications for hospitality and tourism operations. *International Journal of Hospitality Management* 95, 102930. DOI: 10.1016/j.ijhm.2021.102930.

Liu, S. (2020) Artificial intelligence software market revenue worldwide 2018-2025. Available at: https://www.statista.com/statistics/607716/worldwide-artificial-intelligence-market-revenues (accessed 7 December 2020).

Lloyd, K. (2018) Bias amplification in artificial intelligence systems. *ArXiv Preprint ArXiv* 1809.07842. Available at: https://doi.org/10.48550/arXiv.1809.07842

Ma, P., Zhang, Z., Wang, J., Zhang, W., Liu, J. *et al.* (2021) Review on the application of metalearning in artificial intelligence. *Computational Intelligence and Neuroscience* 2021, 1560972. DOI: 10.1155/2021/1560972.

McGloin, C. (2020) Travel chatbots: 5 superb use cases take customer experience to new heights. Available at: https://servisbot.com/travel-chatbots/ (accessed 7 February 2023).

Mordor Intelligence (2021) Robotics market: growth, trends, Covid-19 impact, and forecasts (2021–2026). Available at: https://www.mordorintelligence.com/industry-reports/robotics-market (accessed 7 February 2023).

Nair, S. (2019) 4 ways chatbots are transforming the travel industry. Available at: https://www.haptik.ai/blog/chatbots-for-travel-industry/ (accessed 1 February 2019).

Patil, S. and Kolhe, R. (2021) Sector wise impact of COVID-19 on the Indian economy and implementation of possible strategies for financial recovery. *The International Journal of Innovative Research in Engineering & Multidisciplinary Physical Sciences* 9(3), 29–38.

Pedamkar, P. (2020) Artificial intelligence problems. Available at: https://www.educba.com/artificial-intelligence-problems/ (accessed 21 December 2022).

Pencarelli, T. (2020) The digital revolution in the travel and tourism industry. *Information Technology & Tourism* 22(3), 455–476. DOI: 10.1007/s40558-019-00160-3.

Peranzo, P. (2019) AI assistant: the future of travel industry with the increase of artificial intelligence. Available at: https://www.imaginovation.net/blog/the-future-of-travel-with-the-increase-of-ai/ (accessed 10 April 2019).

Pop, R.-A., Săplăcan, Z., Dabija, D.-C. and Alt, M.-A. (2021) The impact of social media influencers on travel decisions: the role of trust in consumer decision journey. *Current Issues in Tourism* 25(5), 823–843.

Poquet, O. and Laat, M. (2021) Developing capabilities: lifelong learning in the age of AI. *British Journal of Educational Technology* 52(4), 1695–1708. DOI: 10.1111/bjet.13123.

Priyadarshini, A. (2020) 8 ways hoteliers are employing virtual assistants to woo customers. Available at: https://becominghuman.ai/8-ways-hoteliers-are-employing-virtual-assistants-to-woo-customers-e9e0db3ab07a (accessed 19 May 2020).

Research and Markets (2021) Global hotel and other travel accommodation market report 2021: market is expected to grow from $673.02 billion in 2020 to $801.9 billion in 2021 - long-term forecast to 2025 & 2030. Available at: https://www.globenewswire.com/en/news-release/2021/04/01/2203058/28124/en/Global-Hotel-and-Other-Travel-Accommodation-Market-Report-2021-Market-is-Expected-to-Grow-from-673-02-Billion-in-2020-to-801-9-Billion-in-2021-Long-term-Forecast-to-2025-2030.html (accessed 1 April 2021).

Revfine.com (2020) 8 examples of robots being used in the hospitality industry. Available at: https://www.revfine.com/robots-hospitality-industry (accessed 21 December 2022).

Revfine.com (2021) 4 ways facial recognition can be used in the travel industry. Available at: https://www.revfine.com/facial-recognition-travel-industry/ (accessed 17 March 2021).

Rust, R.T. and Huang, M.-H. (2021) *The Feeling Economy: How Artificial Intelligence Is Creating the Era of Empathy*. Springer Nature, Cham. DOI: 10.1007/978-3-030-52977-2.

Samala, N., Katkam, B.S., Bellamkonda, R.S. and Rodriguez, R.V. (2020) Impact of AI and robotics in the tourism sector: a critical insight. *Journal of Tourism Futures* 8(1), 73–87. DOI: 10.1108/JTF-07-2019-0065.

Seyitoğlu, F. and Ivanov, S. (2021) Service robots as a tool for physical distancing in tourism. *Current Issues in Tourism* 24(12), 1631–1634. DOI: 10.1080/13683500.2020.1774518.

Siau, K. and Wang, W. (2020) Artificial intelligence (AI) ethics: ethics of AI and ethical AI. *Journal of Database Management (JDM)* 31(2), 74–87.

Siteminder (2020) The future is now: how robots are storming the travel industry. Available at: https://www.siteminder.com/r/trends-advice/hotel-travel-industry-trends/future-robots-storming-travel-industry/ (accessed 21 December 2022).

Steeves, K. (2019) How to attract travelers with google maps marketing. Available at: https://www.checkfront.com/google-maps-marketing (accessed 6 June 2019).

Trends, T. (2020) The future is now: how robots are storming the travel industry. Available at: https://www.siteminder.com/r/trends-advice/hotel-travel-industry-trends/future-robots-storming-travel-industry/ (accessed 21 December 2022).

Vijai, C. and Wisetsri, W. (2021) Rise of artificial intelligence in healthcare startups in India. *Advances In Management* 14(1), 48–52.

Wendemagegnehu, T.T. (2021) The influence of social media on the travel decisionmaking behavior of Ethiopian educational tourists in Poland: the case of Ethiopian educational tourists in Poland. University essay from Högskolan dalarna/institutionen för kultur och samhälle.

Wu, Z., Ji, D., Yu, K., Zeng, X., Wu, D. *et al.* (2021) AI creativity and the human-AI co-creation model. In: *International Conference on Human-Computer Interaction*, pp. 171–190.

Yu, Z., Liang, Z. and Wu, P. (2021) How data shape actor relations in artificial intelligence innovation systems: an empirical observation from china. *Industrial and Corporate Change* 30(1), 251–267.

Zaino, L. (2020) 9 best translations apps for travellers. Available at: https://thepointsguy.com/guide/best-translation-apps-for-travel (accessed 3 April 2020).

Zaragoza-Sáez, P., Marco-Lajara, B. and Ubeda-Garcia, M. (2021) Digital skills in tourism. A study from the next tourism generation (NTG) alliance. *Measuring Business Excellence* 26(1), 106–121.

Zghyer, F., Yadav, S. and Elshazly, M.B. (2021) Artificial intelligence and machine learning. In: *Precision Medicine in Cardiovascular Disease Prevention*. Springer, pp. 133–148.

Zhang, C. and Lu, Y. (2021) Study on artificial intelligence: the state of the art and future prospects. *Journal of Industrial Information Integration* 23, 100224. DOI: 10.1016/j.jii.2021.100224.

5 The Influence of Instagram on Generation Z Travel Motivation and Destination Choice Making to the Actual Travelling

Kuldeep Verma*, R.K. Dhodi and Rashmi Dhodi

Hemvati Nandan Bahuguna Garhwal University, Srinagar, Uttarakhand, India

Abstract

Purpose: Globally, with one billion active users, Instagram is one of the most popular social media platforms among the younger generation. Generation Z (born between 1995 and 2010), compared to other generations, are more likely to turn to social networks to discover products and get inspired. The purpose of the study was to find out how Gen Z gets motivated and makes their destination choices through user-generated content on Instagram and whether they, in fact, travel to the selected destination.

Design/methodology/approach: The research conducted is based on quantitative methods in the form of an online survey. The survey was done with Google forms and targeted individuals born between 1995 and 2010 residing mainly in the Delhi-NCR region of India. The survey included questions about travel motivation and destination choice through user-generated content on Instagram. The results from the survey were analysed using SPSS and Google forms response statistics.

Findings: According to the study outcome, Instagram does motivate Gen Z for travelling and selecting the destination for travel. However, after viewing the feed on Instagram, the majority of the individuals look for other sources of information for planning their travel. Gen Z does not possess the same wealth as the older generations; therefore, in most cases, the individual's income limit inhibits them from actually travelling to the destination they viewed.

Originality/value: A study was done by Booking.com on Gen Z and social media and concluded that Instagram is the top source of inspiration when it comes to deciding on a vacation destination. The research was limited and did not show the motivation behind deciding on the destination and what percentage of individuals actually travelled to the selected destination, which is covered in this study.

The value of this article is to provide the insight to reach Gen Z (who soon will surpass the millennials, currently the most populous generation, and will count for one third of the world's population) successfully, catch their attention and tap into their needs and desires.

Introduction

Social media has significantly influenced the tourism sector in recent years. Consumers, for example, use social media to research trips, make travel selections, and share their personal travel experiences. Many elements of the tourism industry are changing due to the advances and evolution of social media. Furthermore, they affect tourists' motivation and the entire vacation planning process (Leung *et al.*, 2013).

*Corresponding author: kuldeepvermabhu@gmail.com

© CAB International 2023. *Technology and Social Transformations in Hospitality, Tourism and Gastronomy: South Asia Perspectives* (eds S. Sharma and S. Bhartiya)
DOI: 10.1079/9781800621244.0005

Popular social media sites include Facebook, Twitter, Pinterest, Snapchat, Tripadvisor, LinkedIn and Instagram. Because social media is quite broad, we will be focusing on Instagram due to its increasing popularity among young people. Instagram is a social networking app used predominantly to share pictures and videos from a smartphone. *Social Media Statistics for 2021* (Statusbrew, 2021) reported that Instagram is used by more than 1.2 billion people every month, globally, and with 120 million users India tops the list of number of users. Sixty-seven per cent of users on Instagram are aged 18–29, which largely comprises Gen Z.

Many studies revolve around Gen Z and how social media influences their decision to select a tourist destination or how social media provides information for determining a tourist destination. However, the focal point of these studies is the influence of social media in travel planning and destination choice. New features added on Instagram, like reels, do not provide much information for tourists (some posts do not even mention the destination shown in them), but they might motivate travel. Therefore, this study is all about knowing how Gen Z gets motivated after seeing the feeds on Instagram, what kinds of feeds motivate them, how they choose the destination based on these facts, and how many of them travel to the destination they selected.

Study Objectives

The purpose of the study was to find out how Gen Z gets motivated and makes destination choices through user-generated content on Instagram and whether they, in fact, travel to the selected destination.

Literature Review

Generation Z

Pew Research Centre (Dimock, 2019) determined a cut-off point in 2018 between millennials and the next generation and concluded that anyone born after 1997 belongs to a new generation, i.e. Generation Z. The determination of generational cut-off points is not a precise science; therefore different studies suggested a different year of birth for Gen Z ranging from 1993 to 1997 (Dimock, 2019; Turner, 2015; Seemiller and Grace, 2016; Goh and Lee, 2018). However, 1995–2010 is the most commonly used birth band for studying Gen Z.

Characteristics of Generation Z

According to Francis and Hoefel (2018), members of Generation Z — roughly defined as people born between 1995 and 2010 — are indeed digital natives, having grown up with access to the internet, social media and mobile devices. Francis and Hoefel (2018) conducted a survey in Brazil with Box1824, a consumer trends research organization, to investigate the habits of this new generation and their impact on purchase patterns reveals four key Gen Z habits, all of which are centred on one thing: their quest for truth. Individual expression is valued by Gen Z, which detests labels. They get together to support a range of issues. They are firm believers in the power of conversation to resolve disputes and improve the world. Finally, they are highly analytical and pragmatic in their decision making and interactions with institutions. A study by Sladek and Grabinger (2014) revealed that Gen Z is financially conscious (they read reviews, examine the product online or in person, and scan the internet for the best discounts), globally minded (social media allows them to communicate with individuals around the world) and lack work experience (the majority under the age of 25 have never worked). Unlike previous generations, Gen Z has not been given the opportunity to gain work experience throughout their teenage years. They are tech-savvy.

Generation Z and social media usage

The internet has played a significant role in the lives of Gen Z (Turner, 2015). Today, Gen Z cannot recall life without social media (Fromm and Read, 2018). Although there have been studies on Gen Z's growing social media usage, further study on their social media activities and their behavioural impact are needed. This generation has a strong gravitational link with online communication, wanting to interact and stay linked with technology at their fingertips. They are active contributors and heavy consumers of online information, and are creative and mash-up specialists (Prakash Yadav and Rai, 2017).

Role of social media in tourism and travel

Travellers increasingly use social media to find, organize, share and discuss their travel stories and experiences through different social media platforms (Leung *et al.*, 2013). Social media websites are an important medium for providing travel-related information (Sun *et al.*, 2020). Compared to other information sources, social media provides travellers with a more thorough understanding of a tourism location through first-hand user-generated content (Xiang and Gretzel, 2010). User-generated content (UGC), sharing of photos, videos and reviews/comments with others on social media, will help engage potential tourists who will, in turn, generate greater revenue and help the tourism and hospitality sector to grow (Leung *et al.*, 2013).

Social media, tourist motivation and destination choices

Different studies concluded that social media influences tourist motivation, which in turn influences tourist decision-making behaviour. Due to their predominance on the platforms, the different social networking sites, including Instagram, largely impact the younger generation (Munar and Jacobsen, 2014; Christou, 2016; Huertas, 2018). Given the importance of social media in both tourists' decision making and tourism operations and management, a slew of research on the use of social media in tourism and hospitality has been published in peer-reviewed publications (Xiang and Gretzel, 2010; Chan and Guillet, 2011; Li and Wang, 2011; Noone *et al.*, 2011).

Impact of Instagram on travel motivation and destination choice

A study by Booking.com on Gen Z reveals that when it comes to choosing a holiday destination, Instagram is the most popular source of inspiration among Gen Z. The suggestions of people they do not know in person, such as influencers and celebrities, are trusted by 39% of Gen Z. Almost a quarter (19%) of 'snap happy' Gen Zers take more than 50 photos each day on vacation and love to share them publicly, with 40% posting on social media. However, nearly half (48%) believe that when travelling, too much focus is placed on social media.

Research Methodology

The descriptive research has been implemented in the current study, and the primary data for the research has been collected with the help of an online questionnaire using Google forms.

Gen Z is the subject of this study. Data are collected from individuals residing in the New Delhi region of India who were born between 1995 and 2010.

Following a review of the literature, a questionnaire was developed. The questionnaire was comprised of three parts. The first part dealt with the respondent's basic information; the second section comprised questions about how travel-related feeds motivate the respondent; the third part comprised questions about how Instagram feeds lead to the selection of a destination. The questionnaires contained five-point Likert-scale questions and multiple-choice questions.

A total of 123 questionnaires were received, out of which 100 were valid and considered for analysis in SPSS (rejected questionnaires had missing responses). Simple descriptive analyses were performed to justify the objectives.

To describe respondents' opinions, Likert-scale questions were used: strongly disagree-1, disagree-2, neutral-3, agree-4, and strongly agree-5. In statistics, the mean is critical for describing data on the Likert scale. From 1 to 1.8 the answer is 'strongly disagree', from 1.8 to 2.60 the answer is 'disagree', from 2.61 to 3.40 the answer is 'neutral', from 3.41 to 4.20 the

Table 5.1. How often do you use Instagram?

	Frequency	%	Valid %	Cumulative %
Rarely	4	4	4	4
Once a day	15	15	15	19
4–5 times a day	55	55	55	74
Continuously throughout the day	26	26	26	100
Total	100	100	100	

Source: Author's own work.

Table 5.2. Types of accounts followed.

	Responses		% of cases
	n	%	
Friends/family	90	35.3	90.0
Bloggers/influencers	47	18.4	47.0
Celebrities	40	15.7	40.0
Countries/destinations	34	13.3	34.0
Product brands	27	10.6	27.0
Hotels, restaurants, airlines etc.	17	6.7	17.0
Total	255	100.0	255.0

Source: Author's own work.

answer is 'agree', and from 4.21 to 5 the answer is 'strongly agree'.

Results

Respondent profile

Out of 100 samples, 55 were male and 45 were female. The age of the respondents was between 15 and 26. The age categories and percentages were: 21–22 (30%), 25–26 (29%), 19–20 (19%), 23–24 (16%). Fifty-four per cent had a Bachelor's degree or equivalent followed by a Master's degree or equivalent (25%) and the remainder high school or equivalent. The clear majority of the respondents were students (74%), 9% having private jobs, 8% being unemployed, 4% holding government positions, 3% were freelance and 2% were business owners. As most of the respondents were students, clearly they had low income and were dependent to an extent on parents; 77% of respondents did not have any income; 9% earned less than 1 lakh (IR); 9% earned

between 3 and 5 lakhs; 4% earned between 1 and 3 lakhs; and only 1% earned between 5 and 7 lakhs.

Table 5.1 shows that the majority of the respondents use Instagram daily, 4–5 times (55%), 26% use Instagram throughout the day, 15% use it once a day, and 5% use it rarely.

Table 5.2 shows the types of accounts Gen Z respondents are following. The majority of the respondents follow friends/family, followed by bloggers/influencers and celebrities.

According to Table 5.3, travel-related feeds on Instagram motivate Gen Z to travel (mean = 3.75). Table 5.4 shows that the majority of Gen Z are motivated by the posts showing new experiences/adventures (n=70) followed by posts showing destinations for relaxation (n=59); (n=37) get motivation from other people travelling; (n=37) get motivation after watching destinations on posts where they can explore themselves; (n=34) get motivated after watching exotic destinations on Instagram; (n=30) get inspiration for travelling from the influencers on Instagram. Very few respondents feel pressure to travel

Table 5.3. Travel-related feeds on Instagram motivate me to travel.

n	Minimum	Maximum	Mean	Std deviation
100	1	5	3.75	1.104

Source: Author's own work.

Table 5.4. How travel-related posts on Instagram motivate me to travel.

	Responses		% of cases
	n	%	
Shows exotic destination	34	11.9	34.0
Seeing other people travelling	37	13.0	37.0
Feel pressure to travel after seeing travel posts	10	3.5	10.0
Feeling in competition with peers who are travelling	8	2.8	8.0
Influencer travelling inspires you to travel	30	10.5	30.0
Posts of new experiences/adventures	70	24.6	70.0
Shows destinations for relaxation	59	20.7	59.0
Shows destinations for exploring yourself	37	13.0	37.0
Total	285	100.0	285.0

Source: Author's own work.

Table 5.5. Travel to share on Instagram.

n	Minimum	Maximum	Mean	Std deviation
100	1	5	3.45	1.313

Source: Author's own work.

Table 5.6. How sharing posts motivates travel.

	Responses		% of cases
	n	%	
Increase awareness of what can be experienced	45	21.0	45.0
Like to show the places I have visited	62	29.0	62.0
To get 'likes'	13	6.1	13.0
The perception of having to keep up	11	5.1	11.0
Socially accepted thing to do	21	9.8	21.0
For personal collection	62	29.0	62.0
Total	214	100.0	214.0

Source: Author's own work.

(*n*=10) after seeing the posts and only (*n*=9) travel because their friends on Instagram are travelling.

According to Tables 5.5 and 5.6, Gen Z agreed that they travel to share photos and videos of their journey using Instagram (mean = 3.45) as (*n*=62) respondents like to show the places they have visited. (*n*=45) respondents want to travel to share photos and videos to increase the awareness of what can be experienced at the destination they have visited. (*n*=21) think that sharing on Instagram about their travel is a socially accepted thing to do. Few respondents (*n*=13)

Table 5.7. Type of content on Instagram that motivates travel.

	Responses		% of cases
	n	%	
Beaches	52	15.2	52.0
Tropical island/resorts	39	11.4	39.0
Mountains	84	24.6	84.0
Desert	15	4.4	15.0
Forest	53	15.5	53.0
Cultural attraction	49	14.3	49.0
Monuments/building structures	20	5.8	20.0
Cities	30	8.8	30.0
Total	342	100.0	342.0

Source: Author's own work.

Table 5.8. Form of travel content that influences/motivates.

	Responses		% of cases
	n	%	
Photos	70	28.2	70.0
Videos	60	24.2	60.0
Story	44	17.7	44.0
Reels	54	21.8	54.0
IGTV	20	8.1	20.0
Total	248	100.0	248.0

Source: Author's own work.

want to travel to share on Instagram to get likes. Only ($n=11$) want to travel to share on Instagram to keep up with other people.

Posts featuring mountains ($n=84$) make Gen Z want to travel followed by posts featuring forests ($n=53$), beaches ($n=52$), cultural attractions ($n=49$), tropical islands/resorts ($n=39$) and cities ($n=30$); posts featuring monuments ($n=20$) and deserts ($n=15$) are the least attractive to motivate respondents to travel (Table 5.7).

Table 5.8 shows that travel content in the form of photos ($n=70$) and videos ($n=60$) on Instagram gives motivation for travelling, followed by the newest feature on Instagram, reels ($n=54$). Stories of travel ($n=44$) shared on Instagram by celebrities and influencers also motivate Gen Z. Instagram TV (IGTV) content, which contains long videos, motivates the least.

Table 5.9 shows that 70% of respondents do not actively search for travel-related content on Instagram as few of them follow travel-related accounts. They are influenced by encountering posts featuring travel content while randomly scrolling. In contrast, 30% of respondents search for travel-related content.

According to Table 5.10, the majority of respondents agree that seeing posts of a destination motivates them to visit the place (mean = 3.85); respondents agree that they were determined to travel to the destination (mean = 3.57) and search for information about the destination (mean = 3.80). However, Instagram does not provide sufficient information about the destination (mean = 2.45); the majority of respondents just gain an initial idea from Instagram and gather detailed information from other sources (mean = 3.95). Respondents agreed that influencers

Table 5.9. Search for travel destinations on Instagram.

	Frequency	%	Valid %	Cumulative %
Actively search for travel-related posts on Instagram	30	30	30	30
Do not actively search but get influenced by random travel feeds	70	70	70	100
Total	100	100	100	

Source: Author's own work.

Table 5.10. Destination choice.

	n	Minimum	Maximum	Mean	Std deviation
Seeing a post of a destination makes me want to visit the place	100	1	5	3.85	1.095
After seeing Instagram feeds, I was determined to travel to that destination	100	1	5	3.57	1.103
After seeing Instagram feeds, I am inspired to find more information about the destination	100	1	5	3.80	1.128
Influencers increase the trust for the destination	100	1	5	3.55	1.184
Negative feed about the destination changes my decision	100	1	5	3.14	1.164
Instagram provides sufficient information for choosing the destination	100	1	4	2.45	0.903
Gain the initial idea from Instagram feeds and do my research on the destination from other sources (YouTube, travel website, official website) and then decide on the destination	100	1	5	3.95	0.978

Source: Author's own work.

Table 5.11. Do you travel to the destination you saw on Instagram feeds?

	Never	Rarely	Sometimes	Often	Always	Total
Frequency	18	20	46	15	1	100
%	18.0	20.0	46.0	15.0	1.0	100.0
Valid %	18.0	20.0	46.0	15.0	1.0	100.0
Cumulative %	18.0	38.0	84.0	99.0	100.0	

Source: Author's own work.

increase trust in choosing the destination (mean = 3.55); respondents have a neutral opinion (mean = 3.5) on negative feeds changing their decision about a destination.

Table 5.11 shows that conversion from motivation to selecting a destination to actually travelling happens only sometimes (46%). Twenty per cent and 18% of respondents stated that they rarely and never, respectively, travel to the destinations they selected from Instagram while 15% of respondents often travel to the destination they saw on Instagram.

Table 5.12. Reasons for not travelling to the destination selected.

	Responses		% of cases
	n	%	
Income/budget	59	34.3	59.0
Lack of time	54	31.4	54.0
Procrastination	9	5.2	9.0
Parents' permission	41	23.8	41.0
Peer group	9	5.2	9.0
Total	172	100.0	172.0

Source: Author's own work.

From the above table, respondents only sometimes travel to the destination and Table 5.12 shows various reasons respondents are unable to travel to the destination they selected. The majority of respondents stated that their income/budget (*n*=59) does not allow them to travel, followed by unavailability of time (*n*=54) and parents' permission (*n*=41).

Findings and Conclusion

Instagram and travel motivation

It is evident from the data that Gen Z agreed that travel-related posts on Instagram motivate them to travel. Scrolling on Instagram feeds and finding new adventures, experiences, calm destinations for relaxation, or watching people travel intrigue them, and they want to experience the same. However, they do not feel pressure or want to travel out of competition with friends or people they saw travelling. The various Instagram features play an important role in providing travel content. According to the data analysed, content in the form of photos, videos, reels and stories intrigue Gen Z. Instagram reels, being the newest feature, have a substantial impact in influencing Gen Z (a report by *USA Today* states that short-form viral videos and images on Instagram and Snapchat are quite popular among Gen Z). IGTV, which features full-length videos, is the least-watched Instagram feature for travel content. Content featuring anything related to mountains, like snow-capped peaks, hiking in mountains, riding a motorcycle in the mountains etc., is quite popular among Gen Z. It motivates them the most to travel for new experiences and adventures.

Gen Z are active contributors to social media content and agreed in the study that they want to travel to share pictures and videos on Instagram. It becomes evident that most of the respondents who belong to Gen Z like to share pictures of the places/tourist destinations they have visited. Though sharing pictures is not the primary motive for travelling, as most of the respondents keep the photos/videos for viewing only by themselves and close associates, they are happy maintaining a record of their visit. Gen Z also wants to travel to share with their followers what could be experienced in the destination they are travelling to. Only a few want to travel and share their journey because they feel it is a socially accepted thing. A very strange outcome of the study is that Gen Z are not sharing to get likes and do not want to share because other people are also sharing.

Destination choice

The tourist decision-making process and individual motives appear complementary, implying that they are not totally distinct processes. Brun *et al.* (1997) proposed that motive functions as a stimulant of the decision-making process. Furthermore, visitor motives and decision making appeared to converge as a single process. Social media and its content frequently aid this process. Individuals stated that viewing anything on social media, such as a vacation photo or video of mountains, typically prompts or motivates them to begin the travel planning process (Blackwell *et al.*, 2006).

Although most respondents do not actively go looking on social media for varied information pertaining to tourist locations, many believe that photos they come across on Instagram will certainly impact their travel plans, as many of them want to visit the place they saw on the Instagram feed.

After viewing Instagram feeds, many are inspired to find more information about the destinations. However, they cannot use Instagram as a research tool as it provides little to no information about the destination. Therefore, Instagram acts only as a source of motivation to gain an initial idea about the destinations. For more information, like accessibility, types of accommodation and their tariff, activities to do, etc., most people rely on other sources like travel websites, YouTube and the destination's official website.

Instagram influencers have some impact on influencing the destination choice as their travel content gives some insight into the destination. However, Gen Z do not believe anything 'blindfolded' and carry out their research to reach a conclusion about the content. This is why they are not affected by posts showing the negative image of a destination.

Actual travelling

There are very few occasions when respondents get to travel to the destination they selected, because of lack of income and unavailability of time, as most of Gen Z were aged only 26 at the time of the study. Most of them do not have any source of income for travel, and most of them are still going to school/college and rarely have time to take a vacation (most of the respondents travel less than three times a year). Another thing that hinders them from travelling is not getting permission to travel from their parents as most of them are still dependent on them.

Implication

The first generation born into an online world is now entering the workforce. Gen Z's income will surpass that of millennials by 2031 (Bank of America, 2020); therefore, they will be paying for all parts of their travel. To capture the attention of Gen Z's ready-to-travel mindset, the hospitality industry marketer should have a strong digital presence by building a digital footprint and marketing experiences through display ads and social media.

References

Bank of America (2020) *Gen Z Primer*. Global Research, OK Zoomer.

Blackwell, R., D'Souza, C., Taghian, M., Miniard, P. and Engel, J. (2006) *Consumer Behaviour: An Asia Pacific Approach*. Thomson.

Brun, W., Edland, A.C., Gärling, T., Harte, J.M., Hill, T. *et al*. (1997) *Decision Making: Cognitive Models and Explanations*, Vol. 1. Psychology Press.

Chan, N.L. and Guillet, B.D. (2011) Investigation of social media marketing: how does the hotel industry in Hong Kong perform in marketing on social media websites? *Journal of Travel & Tourism Marketing* 28(4), 345–368. DOI: 10.1080/10548408.2011.571571.

Christou, E. (2016) *Social Media in Travel, Tourism and Hospitality: Theory, Practice and Cases*. Routledge. DOI: 10.4324/9781315609515.

Dimock, M. (2019) Defining generations: where millennials end and generation Z begins. *Pew Research Center* 17(1), 1–7.

Francis, T. and Hoefel, F. (2018) 'True gen': Generation Z and its implications for companies. *McKinsey & Company* 12.

Fromm, J. and Read, A. (2018) *Marketing to Gen Z: The Rules for Reaching This Vast--and Very Different--Generation of Influencers*. AMACOM.

Goh, E. and Lee, C. (2018) A workforce to be reckoned with: the emerging pivotal Generation Z hospitality workforce. *International Journal of Hospitality Management* 73, 20–28. DOI: 10.1016/j.ijhm.2018.01.016.

Huertas, A. (2018) How live videos and stories in social media influence tourist opinions and behaviour. *Information Technology & Tourism* 19(1–4), 1–28. DOI: 10.1007/s40558-018-0112-0.

Leung, D., Law, R., Hoof, H. van and Buhalis, D. (2013) Social media in tourism and hospitality: a literature review. *Journal of Travel & Tourism Marketing* 30(1–2), 3–22. DOI: 10.1080/10548408.2013.750919.

Li, X. and Wang, Y. (2011) China in the eyes of western travelers as represented in travel blogs. *Journal of Travel & Tourism Marketing* 28(7), 689–719. DOI: 10.1080/10548408.2011.615245.

Munar, A.M. and Jacobsen, J.Kr.S. (2014) Motivations for sharing tourism experiences through social media. *Tourism Management* 43, 46–54. DOI: 10.1016/j.tourman.2014.01.012.

Noone, B.M., McGuire, K.A. and Rohlfs, K.V. (2011) Social media meets hotel revenue management: opportunities, issues and unanswered questions. *Journal of Revenue and Pricing Management* 10(4), 293–305. DOI: 10.1057/rpm.2011.12.

Prakash Yadav, G. and Rai, J. (2017) The generation Z and their social media usage: a review and a research outline. *Global Journal of Enterprise Information System* 9(2), 110. DOI: 10.18311/gjeis/2017/15748.

Seemiller, C. and Grace, M. (2016) *Generation Z goes to College*. John Wiley & Sons.

Sladek, S. and Grabinger, A. (2014) *Gen Z. Introducing the First Generation of the 21st Century*. Available at: https://www.xyzuniversity.com/wp-content/uploads/2018/08/GenZ_Final-dl1.pdf (accessed 20 July 2021).

Statusbrew (2021) Social Media Statistics for 2021. Statusbrew Blog. Available at: https://statusbrew.com/insights/social-media-statistics/ (accessed 22 December 2022).

Sun, S., Law, R. and Luk, C. (2020) Tourists' travel-related information search channels. *International Journal of Hospitality & Tourism Administration* 23(2), 149–164. Available at: https://doi.org/10.1080/15256480.2020.1727809 (accessed 22 December 2022).

Turner, A. (2015) Generation Z: technology and social interest. *The Journal of Individual Psychology* 71(2), 103–113. DOI: 10.1353/jip.2015.0021.

Xiang, Z. and Gretzel, U. (2010) Role of social media in online travel information search. *Tourism Management* 31(2), 179–188. DOI: 10.1016/j.tourman.2009.02.016.

Section B: Social Transformation

6 Service Quality Perspective and Guest Satisfaction in Food and Beverage Outlets of Five-star Hotels of Delhi-NCR

Omar Abdullah[1]*, Tahir Sufi[1] and Sanjeev Kumar[2]
[1]Amity School of Hospitality, Amity University, Noida, Uttar Pradesh, India; [2]Institute of Hotel & Tourism Management, Maharshi Dayananda University, Rohtak, Haryana, India

Abstract

The main objective of the present study is to analyse the level of service quality as perceived by guests of food and beverage outlets of five-star hotels. This research offers some positive and constructive suggestions for closing the service gap, as well as preliminary findings based on the SERVQUAL model, which measures the mutual relationships between service quality and guest satisfaction. Quality dimensions have been used to investigate service quality and guest satisfaction, and some recommendations for improving service quality have been made. A sample size of 110 guests was taken into consideration by the food and beverage outlets of five-star hotels of Delhi-NCR to evaluate the model. Interviews and questionnaires were used to acquire primary data. Secondary data were gathered through a review of the literature. The present relationship between service quality and consumer satisfaction is investigated evaluating the above-mentioned responses. The study implies that service quality plays a very important role as a carrier for complete customer satisfaction in hotel restaurant services. It is believed that these findings will further contribute to the industry becoming more aware of customer choices and service quality in order to minimize and handle guest complaints tactfully.

Introduction

Service quality and customer satisfaction are significant for an organization's presence. Both are elusive, however, and their exact depiction remains a matter of debate. Consumer loyalty is a mental idea that alludes to the feeling of joy that comes from getting what one needs and anticipates from an advantageous item or administration. The assumption disconfirmation perspective is utilized to characterize client satisfaction. The most significant aspect of marketing quality that determines restaurant quality and loyalty is people (Kukanja *et al.*, 2017). In today's hospitality situations, the expression 'doing it right the first time' (Ali *et al.*, 2018) still holds true. Anticipating many consumers' decision-making processes, particularly those who evaluate many restaurant-related variables before picking where to dine, could be quite beneficial to restaurateurs, as first impressions are the most important. The restaurant industry has grown to be one of the most lucrative in the world. Customers' demands for a diverse range of products and services are being met by international and local restaurant

*Corresponding author: omarwani93@gmail.com

© CAB International 2023. *Technology and Social Transformations in Hospitality, Tourism and Gastronomy: South Asia Perspectives* (eds S. Sharma and S. Bhartiya)
DOI: 10.1079/9781800621244.0006

businesses. Customer satisfaction is critical for any business, whether it is in the service or private sectors. Customers are the actual agents or stakeholders who determine or best judge a product's or service's success. In the food and beverage industry, a consumer's overall evaluation is linked to both tangible and intangible components of their consuming experiences (Almohaimmeed, 2017). Service quality has three important characteristics, according to Ha and Jang (2010): service quality; discernment quality; and administration quality.

Service quality is significantly harder to quantify than merchandise quality; discernment quality emerges from clients' assumptions and views of genuine help; and administration quality is reflected in the gap between assumptions and impressions of administration experience. According to service literature, the most essential aspects in a consumer's judgement may alter depending on the specific driver that prompts a person to visit a restaurant. In festivities, for example, the quality and variety of food appear to be crucial. When convenience is the primary motivation, location becomes a critical factor, and the restaurant's reputation appears to be an important aspect in both leisure and business outings. The atmosphere is also a consideration on several occasions (Al-Dhaafri and Al-Swidi, 2016). In order to properly create the relationships and habits that lead to true loyalty, restaurants must make strategic decisions about their guest experience approaches. Several measurement frameworks have been developed to study service quality, including SERVQUAL (Parasuraman *et al.*, 1985, 1988), synthesized model of service quality, SERVPERF (Cronin and Taylor, 1992) and the antecedents and mediator model (Ladhari *et al.*, 2008).

From the standpoint of business administration, service quality is a success in customer service. Every interaction with a customer reflects this. Customers form service expectations based on previous experiences, word-of-mouth and marketing messaging. Customers, on the whole, compare perceived and expected service, and they are disappointed when the former falls short. Subjective characteristics of customer service are measured by the consistency of the projected benefit with the perceived result. This, in turn, is contingent on the customer's expectations for the service, as well as the service provider's ability and talent in delivering that service.

In consumer services research and management, the concept of customer experience is becoming increasingly essential. Prior study has looked at restaurant experiences in terms of aspects like meal quality, but additional research is needed to figure out what kind of value people ultimately perceive. In this study, quality attributes are related to value assessments as well as behavioural intent, and the customer value viewpoint is introduced to the restaurant experience. In terms of concept, the study mixes customer-perceived value with more typical service/restaurant experience models. By moving the focus from restaurant quality to consumers' perceptions of value generated from these traits, the study broadens managers' understanding of how to create amazing experiences. Consequently, for management, it becomes essential to examine the strengths and weaknesses of the services rendered.

Several studies have been conducted to explore the area identified after a critical review of the literature, which revealed that very few studies have been undertaken by researchers in the context of service quality perspective and guest satisfaction in food and beverage outlets of five-star hotels in the Indian context, particularly in Delhi-NCR. Many studies undertaken in the West have limited relevance to the Indian hospitality industry. Furthermore, it has been noted that study done on the subject in the literature is quite generic. As a result, in order to close this gap, the current study was undertaken on the applicable issue of service quality perspective and guest satisfaction in food and beverage outlets of five-star hotels of Delhi-NCR.

Literature Review

Food quality and the physical atmosphere affect consumer satisfaction greatly in eateries, and consumer satisfaction is a huge indicator of behavioural intention (Ryu and Han, 2010). Food is the main quality measurement in influencing the client's choice interaction, quality discernment and level of satisfaction, as per various studies (Sulek and Hensley, 2004; Cheng *et al.*, 2012; Kim *et al.*, 2009; Kukanja *et al.*,

2017). The most significant parts of building a strong guest relationship are giving every client singular consideration and understanding their individual requirements (Giebelhausen *et al.*, 2016). Understanding the needs of customers is the initial phase in creating client connections that focus on reliability, maintenance and wide-ranging organizations (Wu and Liang, 2009). The most prominent strategy is to foster happiness and positive expectations among eatery clients' requests, devise how to meet them, and co-ordinate these strategies into functional methods. Hierarchical approaches and staff support are needed, as indicated by Lu *et al.* (2015). Food quality, service and atmosphere are three significant areas that influence a customer's opinion.

The service and atmosphere provided by five-star hotel restaurants both need to be great (Namkung and Jang, 2007). Fine-dining restaurants are relied upon to be unique in relation to ordinary restaurants in almost every way, including the most elevated level of costs with exceptional standards, the best atmosphere and working systems (Heung and Gu, 2012). Three other theoretical quality perspectives – responsiveness, reliability and assurance – greatly affect customer satisfaction. Responsiveness, which alludes to a readiness to serve customers, to react to customer solicitations and adaptability to meet customers' needs, greatly affects consumer satisfaction (Nguyen *et al.*, 2015).

The literature has perceived the pertinence of service quality for corporate execution through the immediate and circuitous consequences for consumer loyalty and satisfaction (Al Khattab and Aldehayyat, 2011). Parasuraman *et al.* (1985) set up the SERVQUAL scale in 1985 by looking at assumptions and insights on ten assistance quality viewpoints. This scale was extended in 1988 to incorporate five service quality dimensions: tangible, reliability, responsiveness, assurance and empathy. These five dimensions are evaluated in a total of 44 items, with 22 items estimating general expectations regarding services and the other 22 items estimating consumers' perceptions about the degree of service really given by the outlet within that classification (Kim *et al.*, 2009). However, SERVQUAL has been criticized for its ambiguity, thus Cronin and Taylor (1992) developed SERVPERF, which only measures

performance in 22 items. In terms of methodology, the SERVPERF scale beats the SERVQUAL scale by halving the number of items and allowing a single-item scale to explain more variance in service quality (Oliver, 1980; Jain and Gupta, 2004). Authenticity is regarded as a virtue and an essential marketing technique for gaining a competitive advantage and promoting a product's success in business (Keith and Simmers, 2011; Lu *et al.*, 2015). Furthermore, customers' views of genuineness, their approach relating to a genuine restaurant, are established on the basis of assessments of the totality of the ethnic cuisine – the cuisine offered, the restaurant's interior and outdoor settings, the mood they experience, and the people they come into contact with (Kim and Ham, 2016). A more authentic restaurant can help in this regard. Potential customers will be able to recognize you readily; you will be accurately identified and they will be satisfied with a meal that is authentic.

A strategy for rendering services that are explicitly recognizable in aspects other than quality is a factor in detemining consumer satisfaction in a given outlet (Giebelhausen *et al.*, 2016). Service quality parameters, for instance, are significant determinants of customer satisfaction and loyalty (Izogo and Ogba, 2015). Both positive and negative feelings related to perceived service quality impact consumer loyalty (Ladhari *et al.*, 2008). The vital factors in boosting or bringing down consumers' views of service quality include worker commitment and atmosphere (As'ad *et al.*, 2018). Service quality affects premium eating across all dimensions, as indicated by (Sahni and Mohsin, 2017).

Food quality has for some time been perceived as a significant part of the general restaurant experience. Food quality is a prominent dimension for meeting customers' demands and expectations. Furthermore, food quality in restaurants has a significant association with customer loyalty and readiness to pay (Njite *et al.*, 2015). Physical, compositional and microbiological properties, technical or storage-induced modifications, nutritional value, and safety are among factors that influence food quality (Trimigno *et al.*, 2015). Customers eat with their eyes first, according to Jain and Gupta (2004), hence changing the visual layout of the meal's components can significantly improve or diminish a diner's experience of the same components. Food novelty, quantity, appearance, menu variety, taste and serving temperature are among the most generally recognized indicators of food quality. Customer satisfaction is influenced by meal presentation, flavour and temperature, but food appearance, taste and healthy options have a significant impact on behavioural intention.

Customer satisfaction and behaviour intention at restaurants are influenced by a variety of factors: customers assess the quality of a restaurant based on four dimensions: people, location, food and physical evidence, all of which have a significant impact on their behaviour after purchasing (Kukanja *et al.*, 2017). According to Wilson *et al.* (2012), the three important elements of the service familiarity are functional cues, mechanical cues (non-human features) and human signals (behaviour). As a result, important restaurant aspects including meal quality, service quality and atmosphere can be evaluated.

Restaurants should perceive their weaknesses and carry out satisfactory functional plans and promotional approaches to further develop consumer loyalty, notwithstanding solid competition (Hsiao *et al.*, 2016). Customer satisfaction is a significant business metric that impacts customer repurchase goals (Edward and Sahadev, 2011). Customer satisfaction predicts repeat business and acquiring new customers and has major monetary consequences for an organization (Tuu and Olsen, 2009; Keshavarz *et al.*, 2016). In the course of the last decade, consumer loyalty has become more prominent in promotional literature, and consumer loyalty research has been more hypothesis-based than most literature (Oh and Kim, 2017). Many quantitative studies have shown that service, food, environment and ambiance are the main components in customers' contentment in restaurants (Brunner *et al.*, 2008; Chin, 1998; Danesh *et al.*, 2012; Bhagat, 2016; Biswas and Verma, 2022).

The hospitality industry has adopted the concept of authenticity in its marketing tactics as a brand-positioning and product-appeal approach for years (Kumar, 2012). Authenticity can be conceptualized if the cuisine and atmosphere depict the ethnic origin's actual or 'true' taste and culture. Consumers only believe their experiences are genuine if they are aware that the locations have been carefully planned (Lebe, 2006). Authenticity is seen as an important marketing tactic for gaining a competitive edge

and promoting corporate success (Lu *et al.*, 2015).

Objective

The study aims at evaluating the concept of service quality and its interactive impacts for customer satisfaction. Further, the study aims at examining the customer's perceptions of service quality in food and beverage outlets of five-star hotels.

Research Methodology

The main purpose of the present study is to evaluate criteria for high levels of service quality that can be used as a standard for determining customer satisfaction in food and beverage outlets of Delhi-NCR's five-star hotels. On the basis of location and affordability, the food and beverage outlets were chosen from a pool of ten well-known five-star chain hotels in the capital: Delhi-NCR.

A sample of 110 respondents was collected, which is sufficient to provide a clear image of the entire population. Through the convenience sampling technique, the required sample was acquired from respondents who experienced these outlets in five-star hotels. The data were gathered from restaurant customers via a self-administered survey, distributed by the researchers. The questionnaire was divided into two sections. Section A dealt with the respondents' demographic profile, which included age, gender, location of residence, education, annual household income, marital status, occupation and frequency of restaurant visits. Customers' expectations with variables were recorded in the second section, B, after they used a restaurant's services. Customers' expectations were measured using a five-point Likert scale, with 5 representing 'strongly agree', 4 as 'agree', 3 as 'neutral', 2 as 'disagree' and 1 as 'strongly disagree'. Secondary data were gathered for this study from a variety of sources, including past research papers published in journals, books, published and unpublished theses, and websites. The questionnaire was created with the help of the literature research, which helped in constructing the variables and selecting the objectives, as well as the analysis and interpretation of the data. For analysing the data, the SPSS version 20 was employed. To determine the study's outcomes, a

Table 6.1. Model summary.

Model	R square	Adjusted R square	Std. error of the estimate
1	0.083	0.013	0.462

Source: Author's own work.
Predictors (constant): What is the main reason to dine out? Current employment status, age range, nationality, level of education completed, marital status, age category

Table 6.2. ANOVA.

ANOVA[a]

	Sum of squares	df	Mean square	F	Sig.
Regression	1.768	7	0.253	1.184	0.320[b]
Residual	19.622	92	0.213		
Total	21.39	99			

Source: Author's own work.
Dependent variable: Do you dine out in food and beverage outlets of five-star hotels?
Predictors (constant): What is the main reason to dine out? Current employment status, age range, nationality, level of education completed, marital status, age category

Table 6.3. Coeffcients.

	Unstandardized coefficients		Standardized coefficients		
	B	Std. error	Beta	T	Sig.
(Constant)	1.037	0.376		2.761	0.007
Age category	−0.188	0.171	−0.262	−1.094	0.277
Age range	0.028	0.017	0.372	1.592	0.115
Level of education completed	−0.035	0.091	−0.04	−0.379	0.706
Marital status	−0.004	0.1	−0.005	−0.045	0.964
Current employment status	0.061	0.086	0.074	0.714	0.477
Nationality	0.223	0.147	0.157	1.511	0.134
What is the main reason to dine out?	−0.039	0.056	−0.074	−0.696	0.488

Source: Author's own work.

variety of statistical methods was used to meet the study's goals, including factor analysis.

Data Analysis and Interpretation

Various statistical techniques were used to examine the data. The findings of the analysis, as well as their interpretation, are presented in Tables 6.1–6.9.

Demographic profile of the respondents

Dependent variable: Do you dine out in food and beverage outlets of five-star hotels?

When we asked consumers if they prefer to eat at five-star restaurants, they responded in a variety of ways, depending on the circumstances. When it comes to age groupings, the elderly prefer less five-star eating, whilst

Table 6.4. Model summary.

Model	R square	Adjusted R square	Std. error of the estimate
1	0.105	−0.007	0.599

Source: Author's own work.

Table 6.5. ANOVA.

	Sum of squares	Df	Mean square	F	Sig.
Regression	3.712	11	0.337	0.94	0.507[a]
Residual	31.598	88	0.359		
Total	35.31	99			

Source: Author's own work.
[a]Predictors (constant): What is the main reason to dine out? Current employment status, age range, nationality, level of education completed, marital status, age category

Table 6.6. Coefficient.

	Unstandardized coefficients		Standardized coefficients		
	B	Std. error	Beta	T	Sig.
(Constant)	0.658	0.454		1.448	0.151
Age category	0.04	0.094	0.044	0.427	0.671
What keeps customers coming back is the quantity, quality and fair price of food and beverage items	0.063	0.097	0.068	0.657	0.513
Politeness, attentiveness, sympathy, and courtesy are all attributes that contribute to guest pleasure and retention	0.153	0.142	0.109	1.076	0.285

Source: Author's own work.
[a]Predictors (constant): What is the main reason to dine out? Current employment status, age range, nationality, level of education completed, marital status, age category

Table 6.7. Model summary.

Model	R square	Adjusted R square	Std. error of the estimate
1	0.02	−0.011	0.596

Source: Author's own work.

the younger generation frequents them. The same can be stated for the guests' educational level and marital status; married people prefer this approach less. This factor is also inversely related to the guests' employment and financial situation. Nationality has a huge impact as well. This appears to be a widespread practice among Indian travellers, based on the responses we've received.

Predictors: (constant)

The predictors were as follows. Attentiveness of the staff serving you is the key factor for guest satisfaction. Employees are aware of specific requirements of customers. Do you think that food and beverage outlets of five-star hotels meet expectations? Politeness, attentiveness, sympathy and courtesy are all

Table 6.8. ANOVA.

	Sum of squares	df	Mean square	F	Sig.
Regression	0.69	3	0.23	0.648	0.586[a]
Residual	34.06	96	0.355		
Total	34.75	99			

Source: Author's own work.
[a]Predictors (constant): What is the main reason to dine out? Current employment status, age range, nationality, level of education completed, marital status, age category

Table 6.9. Coefficients.

	Unstandardized coefficients		Standardized coefficients		
	B	Std. error	Beta	T	Sig.
(Constant)	0.692	1.05		0.659	0.512
Age range	−0.015	0.022	−0.163	−0.697	0.488
Do you think that food and beverage outlets of five-star hotels are meeting expectations?	0.607	0.388	0.588	1.565	0.121
I feel so much happier when the staff greet me, remember my name and know my likes about the food.	0.138	0.121	0.142	1.141	0.257
I am satisfied with the facilities provided by the food and beverage outlets of the five-star hotel.	0.003	0.107	0.003	0.029	0.977
Employees are aware of specific requirements of customers.	−0.053	0.094	−0.059	−0.561	0.576
Staff are capable of providing the promised service in a timely and accurate manner.	−0.455	0.389	−0.451	−1.17	0.245
I get very much attracted to any food outlet of five-star hotels when I see a variety of food and beverage items on the menu card.	0.126	0.125	0.111	1.006	0.317
What keeps customers coming back is the quantity, quality and fair price of food and beverage items.	0.026	0.102	0.028	0.258	0.797
Politeness, attentiveness, sympathy and courtesy are all attributes that contribute to guest pleasure and retention.	0.03	0.146	0.022	0.208	0.836
Age category	0.044	0.214	0.048	0.204	0.838
Attentiveness of the staff serving you is the key factor for guest satisfaction.	0.015	0.023	0.074	0.638	0.525

Source: Author's own work.

attributes that contribute to guests' pleasure and retention. What keeps customers coming back is the quantity, quality and the fair price of food and beverage items. I get very much attracted to any food outlet of a five-star hotel when I see a variety of food and beverage items on the menu card. I am satisfied with the facilities provided by the food and beverage outlets of the five-star hotel. I feel so happy when the staff greet me, remember my name and know my likes about the food. Staff are capable of providing the promised service in a timely and accurate manner.

Dependent variable: Have you ever been impressed by a five-star hotel's food and beverage services?

Predictors: (constant)

The predictors were as follows. Attentiveness of the staff serving you is the key factor for guest satisfaction. Employees are aware of specific requirements of customers, Do you think that food and beverage outlets of five-star hotels meet expectations? Politeness, attentiveness, sympathy and courtesy are all attributes that contribute to guests' pleasure and retention. What keeps customers coming back is the quantity, quality and fair price of food and beverage items. I get very much attracted to any food outlet of a five-star hotel when I see a variety of food and beverage items on the menu card. I am satisfied with the facilities provided by the food and beverage outlets of the five-star hotel. I feel so happy when the staff greet me, remember my name and know my likes about the food. Staff are capable of providing the promised service in a timely and accurate manner.

Dependent variable: Staff are capable of providing the promised service in a timely and accurate manner?

Customers praise the staff's demeanour, which is kind and attentive, and they are more compassionate and courteous to visitors. As a result, people keep coming back to the eatery. As evidenced by the favourable feedback received from customers, the menu's quality, quantity and fair price all contribute to this.

Predictors: (constant)

Politeness, attentiveness, sympathy and courtesy are all attributes that contribute to guests' pleasure and retention. What keeps customers coming back is the quantity, quality and fair price of food and beverage items.

Customers are satisfied when their expectations are met, when they are greeted and handled properly by employees, and when they are wowed by the numerous amenities on offer at five-star establishments, according to the research.

However, because the personnel are unaware of the guests' individual needs, they are unable to perform the promised services in a timely and precise manner, resulting in dissatisfaction among the visitors.

Customers choose restaurants with a diverse menu and a good combination of quantity, quality and fair pricing of food goods, according to our findings. When it comes to guest satisfaction and retention, employee characteristics and behaviour play a big role.

When asked if the staff can provide timely and accurate service, 80% of respondents strongly disagreed that they had ever received timely service in a five-star hotel's food and beverage outlets (Fig. 6.1). Additionally, less than 5% of guests agreed that they had received quick and accurate service. The frequency of the 5 point Likert scale was used to detect and measure the visitor response, as seen in the

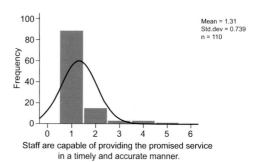

Fig. 6.1. Staff are capable of providing the promised service in a timely and accurate manner. Source: Author's own work.

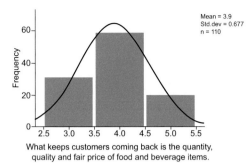

Mean = 3.9
Std.dev = 0.677
n = 110

What keeps customers coming back is the quantity, quality and fair price of food and beverage items.

Fig. 6.2. What keeps customers coming back is the quantity, quality and fair price of food and beverage items.
Source: Author's own work.

histogram below. A strong disagreement is represented by 1 while a strong agreement is represented by 5.

Guests were asked if food price, quality and quantity affect customer retention, or if a food and beverage outlet can be recommended to family and friends while considering all of these factors, but the results show that food price and quantity have no impact on customer retention, but service quality does (Fig. 6.2).

Conclusion

Customers have high expectations when it comes to service, especially in restaurants, because they demand a higher level of service in order to be happy and create a long-term relationship. Food and beverage managers must constantly enhance their service standards, provide training to their personnel, and make their food look and taste excellent in order to maximize profitability and boost organizational performance. Further research is needed to understand how food and beverage service businesses create a complex system of food and beverage service practices in order to understand how these varied practices work together in harmony. Demographic variables and customer satisfaction from food and beverage practices have a significant link. Out of the five demographic variables studied, only gender and income had a positive impact on

the food and beverage service dimensions, according to the researcher. As a result, just a few demographic indicators appear to have a direct impact on consumer happiness. The key to success in satisfying the client is to be attentive. Because prompt service is valued by the guest, the staff must ensure that orders are taken on time and that food is delivered to the guest at a certain time. Customers' behavioural intentions change as a result of customer satisfaction.

This empirical evidence clearly demonstrates both intrinsic and extrinsic relationships between the factors considered in the original proposed model. According to the findings of this study, the quality of the food is the most important element influencing customer happiness and intent to return to the restaurant. As a result, it is strongly advised that restaurant management organize special workshops to provide training to their staff members so that the restaurant may perform better and increase the service quality of the food elements. Because the food and beverage industry has grown at a rapid rate over the previous decade, restaurant managers must be aware of consumer perceptions and service quality criteria such as Physical, People, Convenience, Reliability, Responsiveness, Food, Cleanliness, and Individual Attention. These service quality criteria are important in fast-service restaurants to assess customer views and their intent to return to the same location.

Recommendations

Food and beverage establishments must move from traditional to modern service techniques in order to keep up with technological advancements, consumer expectations and competitiveness. Because the service business is one in which employees and customers interact frequently, it is critical for food and beverage outlets to choose educated professionals with a pleasant demeanour in order to provide personalized service to their guests. To improve customer satisfaction, the restaurant's management should focus on training their employees in the areas of reliability, responsiveness and individual attention.

The purpose of this study was to look into the quality of service and customer satisfaction in five-star hotel restaurants. Physical, People, Convenience, Reliability, Responsiveness, Food, Cleanliness, and Individual Attention were recognized as eight different factors in the study.

Despite its limits, this study will give a platform for improving service quality and customer happiness in the field of five-star hotel restaurants in Delhi-NCR, as well as the formulation of a new agenda for improving service quality and revisiting customer intentions. Many service-related businesses have realized the need for service quality in order to thrive in a competitive world, gain profit and market share, and please customers, despite the fact that these companies have improved their service quality by doing research to determine their service quality shortcomings.

References

Al-Dhaafri, H.S. and Al-Swidi, A. (2016) The impact of total quality management and entrepreneurial orientation on organizational performance. *International Journal of Quality & Reliability Management* 33(5), 597–614.

Ali, F., Kim, W.G., Li, J. and Jeon, H.M. (2018) Make it delightful: customers: customer's experience, satisfaction, and loyalty in Malay. *Journal of Desination Marketing & Management* 7(1), 11.

Al Khattab, S.A. and Aldehayyat, J.S. (2011) Perceptions of service quality in Jordanian hotels. *International Journal of Business and Management* 6(7), 226–233. DOI: 10.5539/ijbm.v6n7p226.

Almohaimmeed, B.M. (2017) Restaurant quality and customer satisfaction. *International Review of Management and Marketing* 7(3), 42–49.

As'ad, H.A., Malkawi, M.S., Lkurdi, B.H. and Alshamaileh, M.O. (2018) Tourist perception toward food and beverage service quality and its impact on behavioral intention: evidence from eastern region hotels in Emirate of Sharjahin United Arab Emirates. *European Journal of Social Sciences* 56(3), 271–282.

Biswas, A. and Verma, R.K. (2022) Augmenting service quality dimensions: mediation of image in the Indian restaurant industry. *Journal of Foodservice Business Research* 1–32.

Brunner, T.A., Stöcklin, M. and Opwis, K. (2008) Satisfaction, image and loyalty: new versus experienced customers. *European Journal of Marketing* 1095–1195.

Cheng, C.C., Chen, C.T., Hsu, F.S. and Hu, H.Y. (2012) Enhancing service quality improvement strategies of fine-dining restaurants: new insights from integrating a two-phase decision-making model of IPGA and DEMATEL analysis. *International Journal of Hospitality Management* 31(4), 1155–1166. DOI: 10.1016/j.ijhm.2012.02.003.

Chin, W. (1998) The partial least square approach for structural equation modeling. In: Marcoulides, G.A. (ed.) *Modern Methods for Business Research*. Lawrence Erlbaum Associates, Hillsdale, NJ, pp. 295–336.

Cronin, J.J. and Taylor, S.A. (1992) Measuring service quality: a reexamination and extension. *Journal of Marketing* (3), 55–68.

Danesh, S., Nasab, S. and Ling, K. (2012) The study of customer satisfaction, customer trust and switching barriers on customer retention in Malaysia hypermarkets. *International Journal of Business and Management* 7(7), 141–150.

Edward, M. and Sahadev, S. (2011) Role of switching costs in the service quality, perceived value, customer satisfaction and customer retention linkage. *Asia Pacific Journal of Marketing and Logistics* 23(3). DOI: 10.1108/13555851111143240.

Giebelhausen, M., Chan, E. and Sirianni, N.J. (2016) Fitting restaurant service style to brand image for greater customer satisfaction. *Cornell Hospitality Report* 16(9), 3–10.

Ha, J. and Jang, S.C.S. (2010) Effects of service quality and food quality: the moderating role of atmospherics in an ethnic restaurant segment. *International Journal of Hospitality Management* 3, 520–529.

Heung, V.C.S. and Gu, T. (2012) Influence of restaurant atmospherics on patron satisfaction and behavioral intentions. *International Journal of Hospitality Management* 31(4), 1167–1177. DOI: 10.1016/j.ijhm.2012.02.004.

Hsiao, Y.H., Chen, L.F., Chang, C.C. and Chiu, F.H. (2016) Configurational path to customer satisfaction and stickiness for a restaurant chain using fuzzy set qualitative comparative analysis. *Journal of Business Research* 69(8), 2939–2949. DOI: 10.1016/j.jbusres.2015.12.063.

Izogo, E.E. and Ogba, I.E. (2015) Service quality, customer satisfaction and loyalty in automobile repair services sector. *International Journal of Quality & Reliability Management* 32(3), 250–269. DOI: 10.1108/IJQRM-05-2013-0075.

Jain, S.K. and Gupta, G. (2004) Measuring service quality: SERVQUAL vs. servperf scales. *Vikalpa* 29(2), 25–38. DOI: 10.1177/0256090920040203.

Keith, N.K. and Simmers, C.S. (2011) Measuring service quality perceptions of restaurant experiences: the disparity between comment cards and DINESERV. *Journal of Foodservice Business Research* 14(1), 20–32. DOI: 10.1080/15378020.2011.548209.

Keshavarz, Y., Jamshidi, D. and Bakhtazma, F. (2016) The influence of service quality on restaurants: customer loyalty. *Arabian Journal of Business and Management Review* 34(3967), 1–16.

Kim, E. and Ham, S. (2016) Restaurants' disclosure of nutritional information as a corporate social responsibility initiative: customers' attitudinal and behavioral responses. *International Journal of Hospitality Management* (C), 96–106.

Kim, W.G., Ng, C.Y.N. and Kim, Y. (2009) Influence of institutional DINESERV on customer satisfaction, return intention, and word-of-mouth. *International Journal of Hospitality Management* 28(1), 10–17. DOI: 10.1016/j.ijhm.2008.03.005.

Kukanja, M., Gomezelj Omerzel, D. and Kodrič, B. (2017) Ensuring restaurant quality and guests' loyalty: an integrative model based on marketing (7P) approach. *Total Quality Management & Business Excellence* 28(13–14), 1509–1525. DOI: 10.1080/14783363.2016.1150172.

Kumar, K.S. (2012) Expectations and perceptions of passengers on service quality with reference to public transport undertakings. *The I.U.P. Journal of Operations Management* XI(3), 67–81.

Ladhari, R., Brun, I. and Morales, M. (2008) Determinants of dining satisfaction and post-dining behavioral intentions. *International Journal of Hospitality Management* 27(4). DOI: 10.1016/j.ijhm.2007.07.025.

Lebe, S.S. (2006) European spa world. *Journal of Quality Assurance in Hospitality & Tourism* 137–146.

Lu, A.C.C., Gursoy, D. and Lu, C.Y. (2015) Authenticity perceptions, brand equity and brand choice intention: the case of ethnic restaurants. *International Journal of Hospitality Management* 50, 36–45.

Namkung, Y. and Jang, S. (2007) Does food quality really matter in restaurants? Its impact on customer satisfaction and behavioral intentions. *Journal of Hospitality and Tourism Research* (3), 387–410.

Nguyen, M., Ha, N., Anh, P. and Matsui, Y. (2015) Service quality and customer satisfaction: a case study of hotel industry in Vietnam. *Asian Social Science* 11. DOI: 10.5539/ass.v11n10p73.

Njite, D., Njoroge, J., Parsa, H., Parsa, R. and van der Rest, J.P. (2015) Consumer patronage and willingness-to-pay at different levels of restaurant attributes: a study from Kenya. *Research in Hospitality Management* 5(2), 171–180. DOI: 10.1080/22243534.2015.11828342.

Oh, H. and Kim, K. (2017) Customer satisfaction, service quality, and customer value: years 2000–2015. *International Journal of Contemporary Hospitality Management* 29(1), 2–29. DOI: 10.1108/IJCHM-10-2015-0594.

Oliver, R.L. (1980) A cognitive model of the antecedents and consequences of satisfaction decisions. *Journal of Marketing Research* 27, 460–469. DOI: 10.1177/002224378001700405.

Parasuraman, A., Zeithaml, V.A. and Berry, L.L. (1985) A conceptual model of service quality and its implications for future research. *Journal of Marketing* 49(4), 41–50. DOI: 10.1177/002224298504900403.

Parasuraman, A., Zeithaml, V.A. and Berry, L.L. (1988) SERVQUAL: a multiple-item scale for measuring consumer perceptions of service quality. *Journal of Retailing* 64(Spring), 12–37.

Ryu, K. and Han, H. (2010) Influence of the quality of food, service, and physical environment on customer satisfaction and behavioral intention in quick-casual restaurants: moderating role of perceived price. *Journal of Hospitality & Tourism Research* (3), 310–329.

Sahni, S. and Mohsin, F. (2017) Factors influencing the selection of fine dining restaurant in Delhi & N.C.R.: an empirical study. *International Journal of Research and Innovation in Social Science (IJRISS)* 1(4), 16–22.

Sulek, J.M. and Hensley, R.L. (2004) The relative importance of food, atmosphere and fairness of wait. *The Cornell Hotel and Restaurant Administration Quarterly* 45(3), 235–247.

Trimigno, A., Marincola, F.C., Dellarosa, N., Picone, G. and Laghi, L. (2015) Definition of food quality by NMR-based foodomics. *Current Opinion in Food Science* 4, 99–104. DOI: 10.1016/j.cofs.2015.06.008.

Tuu, H.H. and Olsen, S.O. (2009) Food risk and knowledge in the satisfaction–
    repurchase loyalty relationship. *Asia Pacific Journal of Marketing and Logistics* 21(4), 521–536. DOI:
    10.1108/13555850910997571.
Wilson, A., Zeithaml, V.A., Bitner, M.J. and Gremler, D.D. (2012) *Services Marketing: Integrating Customer
    Focus across the Firm*, 2nd edn. McGraw-Hill, Maidenhead, UK.
Wu, C.H. and Liang, R. (2009) Effect of experiential value on customer satisfaction with service encounters
    in luxury-hotels restaurants. *International Journal of Hospitality Management* 28, 586–593.

7 Exploring the Indicators of International Tourists' Experience on Local Food of Delhi

Sidharth Srivastava[1]*, Teena Pareek[1] and Savita Sharma[2]
[1]School of Management, JECRC University, Jaipur, India; [2]Skill Faculty of Management Studies & Research, Shri Vishwakarma Skill University, Gurugram, India

Abstract

Food plays a vital role in the tourism industry and attracts many international and domestic tourists. Many tourist destinations promote local food to attract international tourists. With the ease of internet usage, tourists can search for and identify details of local food. The aim of this paper is to identify the determinants of international tourist experience on Delhi's local street food. A total of 443 reviews were collected from Tripadvisor.com, a popular review website in the tourism industry. Of the reviews, 265 were written by international tourists about Delhi street food. Qualitative analysis was performed using R software. Bigram analysis was applied to calculate the repeated phrases. Based on terms, the researchers identified the dimensions. The findings suggested that local food tours, guide behaviour, memorable food experiences, food quality, recommendations, service quality and education were the indicators of tourist experience of Delhi's local food. This study uses the novel dataset. The findings add to the food literature. Further study can be done using big data in different geographical settings.

Introduction

Culinary tourism affords the opportunity for an individual to come out of their daily routine activities and step into the world of food. The demand for culinary tourism is gaining strength and acquiring a pivotal space in the travel and tourism sector. Tourists are stepping out to discover authentic delicacies of a region, not only within the boundaries of a city but also crossing borders. People with the motivation or desire to experience the local food at a destination are known as culinary, food or gastronomy tourists (Cheung, 2009). Nowadays, consumption of local traditional food is becoming a physical requirement and a social activity. While tourists have culinary experiences at a destination, they satisfy their hunger and curiosity to understand the local culture and gain knowledge about food, and the intention to revisit is strengthened. Food was considered a point of attraction for only a few tourists earlier, but now, for more than half of all travellers, it is considered a vital component in the selection of a destination (Seaman *et al.*, 2014).

This indicates that good food is a driving force, even above attractions, architecture and sightseeing (Tsai and Wang, 2017). The passion to try out new regional, authentic, local food is acting as a revival force for culinary customs.

**Corresponding author: sidharthsrivastava2011@yahoo.in

© CAB International 2023. *Technology and Social Transformations in Hospitality, Tourism and Gastronomy: South Asia Perspectives* (eds S. Sharma and S. Bhartiya)
DOI: 10.1079/9781800621244.0007

The local cuisine of a destination is being used to create an intention among tourists to revisit. A lot of tourists are now interested in the origin of food, methods of cooking it, its taste, flavour and ingredients (Lee *et al.*, 2015). Moreover, with the increasing demand for food tourism at a niche level, several agencies and operators are taking advantage by offering local food options to tourists.

Culinary tourism is gaining popularity in several destinations, especially in regions like Asia, North America and Europe. It is found that local delicacies improve the destination's image and sometimes become a distinct characteristic of the place of origin (Ellis *et al.*, 2018). Food acts as an ambassador to portray a country's image and overcome cultural barriers (Choe and Kim, 2019). Culinary tourism attracts tourists and helps other businesses flourish, including kiosks, food outlets, hotels, restaurants, dairy, retail, etc. Food is also considered as a destination marketing tool and it benefits the country's infrastructure and economy (Hwang *et al.*, 2018). It is also found in the literature that food is considered a vital component in travel and accounts for higher traveller expenditure (Brown *et al.*, 2002).

Food that has a historical background, cultural connection, and displays a country's traditions and ethnic customs is a point of interest for tourists (Tsai, 2016). Culinary tourism will be enhanced when the key motive of tourists is curiosity for regional products. Tourists who fall into the category of 'higher interest group' visit a destination to try particular dishes, experience the services of a specific restaurant, participate in food festivals or visit local food markets.

Psychological needs motivate a traveller to travel and eat local food at a distant destination (Fields, 2002). Moreover, it is important to understand the concept of psychological concerns of tourists in order to enhance their experience with local food at a destination. Several studies have shown the importance of specific components – benefits from food, food value, motivational factors, food preferences, and intention to visit. To develop a strong culinary tourism circle, the attention to and the analysis of such components are important. This will contribute to clear recognition of tourist intentions in the future following their experiences at a new destination. Studies also portray the direct link of intention of revisiting to the quality of local food available at a destination (Kim *et al.*, 2018; Stone *et al.*, 2018).

It is also found that the appearance, taste and aroma of the local food lead to higher consumption. Attributes like freshness, quality, taste, cleanliness and aroma attract tourists to a place. The feedback after the consumption of local traditional food generally is positive as the experience of the tourist satisfies his/her culinary motivation and curiosity. Culinary tourists reveal that experiencing food in its country of origin is a unique experience. The urge to taste unknown cuisines and authentic local flavours is always an important point of consideration when selecting a destination (Goolaup and Mossberg, 2017).

The study utilizes digital evidence in the form of online reviews written by tourists after experiencing services at an attraction. These reviews are the best reflectors of their behaviour and interest. Social network profiling of destinations and online reviews can generate interest among tourists so that they can choose the attraction with self-spotted interest (Hernández *et al.*, 2018). Social media and the internet also play a vital role in supporting culinary experience by providing an introduction to food patterns at a destination (Hindley and Wall, 2018). Tourists spend most of the time reviewing products online in order to witness the best culinary experience (Hendijani, 2016). Tourists are also influenced through culinary TV shows, online blogs and various magazines (Wang, 2011; Holmberg *et al.*, 2016). With such an influential background, there is evidence that most culinary tourism research is based on European countries (Duarte Alonso, 2010).

Asia is emerging with unique culinary varieties and warrants research immediately. India has developed itself as a major attraction for culinary tourists because of its traditions and cultural background, but research in the culinary market of India from an international perspective is still limited.

The culinary tourism market, globally, is expected to increase 9% during the period 2019–2023 (www.businesswire.com). Tourists have started to explore food and beverage history, origin and methods. Moreover, with organic products being used in culinary practices, several destinations have become niche markets. Soon, the culinary tourism market will be considered the most important by tourists when selecting a destination. Since the behaviour and attitude of tourists is influenced by social media (Nair, 2017), it becomes important to monitor the feedback of customers through online portals (Tamrakar *et al.*, 2018) and to study the culinary experiences of the international tourist who is crossing borders in search of food.

The term 'culinary' is not restricted to food colour, texture, taste and flavour but also applies to the sentiments attached to food. The purpose behind this study is to evaluate the culinary experiences of the international tourist in order to identify and bridge the gap between their experiences and their expectations.

Delhi, being the capital of India, attracts a lot of tourists who want to experience the city's old culture, heritage, and regional and ethical values. Delhi has gained popularity because of its restricted avenues, ancient havelies, vivid bazaars, and Afgan-/Mughal-inspired traditions and customs. While other states are struggling to attract tourists, Delhi, as the gateway for international tourists, does not require much effort and has always counted as the leading destination for tourism in India. Since its inception, Delhi has had a great combination of cuisines, traditional values, customs and communities. In the last two decades, Delhi has significantly developed its infrastructure, markets, transportation, accommodation and eating venues to facilitate tourism.

To engage tourists, Delhi hosts several festivals related to food and beverages, in order to make itself the preferred culinary destination. Delhi does not have a cuisine of its own but accepts a variety of famous dishes consumed in several other parts of India and the world. The common factor that connects the overcrowded streets of old Delhi with the tiny streets of the other parts and the bazaars is food. Over time, Delhi has delivered a wide range of cuisines, i.e. north Indian, south Indian, Konkan, Mahrashtrian, Rajasthani, Bangoli etc., to satisfy the palate of a large number of tourists/workers in Delhi. Street food there has created its own identity by experimenting with global flavours in a very simple way.

Literature Review

Culinary tourism is also referred to as gastronomy tourism, food tourism, gourmet tourism, tasting tourism and several other terms in the available tourism literature (Horng and Tsai, 2012). Broadly, culinary tourism is defined as movement of people from one place to another in search of food; it can be for the purchase or consumption of food, experiencing local delicacies, food-related festivals, or food cooked by celebrity chefs. Profiles of tourists under culinary tourism have different categories, from the tourist who travels with the prime motive of trying some different food to the tourist who is not interested in food (Andersson *et al.*, 2017). The availability of local food or cuisine is considered an important factor that enhances the tourist experience and builds intention to revisit the destination (Silkes *et al.*, 2013). It is also found that to have a clear understanding of the culture of a destination, one should try the local food (Suntikul, 2019).

Culinary tourism is built on the concepts of interest and necessity which is shown in Table 7.1. The culinary products and services offered at a destination make it unique in comparison to others (Okumus *et al.*, 2007). Experiencing local food at a destination is also a source of entertainment as it includes trying out something new for the first time (Sparks *et al.*, 2003).

Food can be an important point of attraction for a destination if marketed appropriately on social media platforms. Unique marketing strategies can create a positive image in the minds of tourists. The decisions of tourists are influenced by internal as well as external factors (Moutinho, 1987). Demography, technology and consumption ethics are considered the most vital factors that influence culinary tourism (Cohen *et al.*, 2014). Adequate marketing of all the destination's attractions can give a distinct identity to the culture and heritage of the place and can strengthen the economic conditions and improve the sense of competition (Vengesayi *et al.*, 2009). So effective management of tourists' experiences and marketing the destination's attractions to them are crucial. Identifying and connecting the tourist to the destination using online marketing will create a network that can be studied using several

Table 7.1. Previous studies.

Author	Purpose	Methodology	Findings
Correia *et al*., 2020	To study the impact of gastronomy attributes on revisit intention	Fuzzy set analysis	Four attributes were identified which impact revisit intention: food quality, food tradition, uniqueness, and service quality.
Rodrigues, 2020	To study the impact of different local food satisfaction on word-of-mouth (WoM)	Partial least squares structural equation modelling (PLS-SEM)	The authors studied the full mediation, partial mediation and mediation moderation models. All models are significant and have positive effect on word-of-mouth.
Fusté-Forné, 2020	What dimensions are promoted by New Zealand print media with respect to food tourism?	Qualitative study: discourse analysis	Three topics were identified: international practices, regional development, and food culture.
Stone *et al*., 2022	To study the impact of culinary tourism activities on behavioural attitudes of tourists: intention to recommend, revisit intention, and satisfaction	Descriptive statistics	Culinary tourists agreed that satisfied experience impacts revisit intentions, WoM, and economic development of host cities.
Agyeiwaah *et al*., 2019	To understand the relationship between antecedents and outcomes of culinary tourists' experiences: motivation, experience, satisfaction and loyalty	Structure equation modelling	Motivation, experience and satisfaction positively impact loyalty. Experience and satisfaction partially mediate the relationship between motivation and loyalty.
Okumus *et al*., 2018	To understand the culinary tourism marketing strategies of Istanbul tourism	Content analysis	The authors concluded that, despite having international and local cuisines, Istanbul failed to promote itself as a culinary destination.
Chang and Mak, 2018	To extract the gastronomy image dimensions	Content analysis	Seven dimensions, which include 46 attributes, were identified.
Stone *et al*., 2018	To find the determinants of memorable culinary tourism experience	Content analysis	Five broad categories were identified: location or setting, experience related to food or drink, occasion, companionship and tourist elements.

Continued

Table 7.1. Continued

Author	Purpose	Methodology	Findings
Kim *et al.*, 2019	To find the determinants of local food experiences	Content analysis	Three categories were identified: motivational factors, demographic factors and physiological factors.
Tsai and Wang, 2017	To understand the relationship between experiential value, place and food image on behavioural intention of food tourists	Structure equation modelling	The experiential value has positive impact on place food image. Place food image positively impacts behavioural intention of tourists.

theories and analysis (Hernández *et al.*, 2018). As social media affects consumption patterns, behaviour and attitudes, destination managers and agencies are encouraged to evaluate tourist experiences on social media platforms (Tamrakar *et al.*, 2018).

Most of the available literature about the social media impact of marketing on tourism destinations deals with online reviews, satisfaction levels, intention to revisit, purchasing power, preferences (Schuckert *et al.*, 2015) and how destination managers or hospitality business owners can benefit from it to enhance the destination's food image (Leung *et al.*, 2013). Several authors have identified the significant relationship between sales and online reviews, which is an important indicator to develop a business (Ye *et al.*, 2009). Quality of the content of reviews, the information provided, customer satisfaction level and the website's reputation can contribute to building consumer trust in the review (Filieri *et al.*, 2015). Emotions analysis, topic modelling, polarity, hashtag analysis and several other approaches are being used to study online reviews (Aswani *et al.*, 2018). Much of the research pertaining to online portals, Google Maps and Lonely Planet has been analysed, giving a new dimension to the methods of analysis (Chuang *et al.*, 2017). There are several advantages associated with analysing the data online, like easy availability, accuracy, freedom from bias etc. Online reviews are generally in a form called big data and are difficult to analyse with traditional research tools (Guo *et al.*, 2017). In the last decade, the number of tourists giving their feedback on online portals has increased dramatically. Most products like

food, accommodation, transportation, culture and activities are difficult to judge before actually experiencing them (Simeon *et al.*, 2017). So users have started referring to online reviews to gain an image of the destination (Filieri *et al.*, 2015). Nowadays, tourists often share experiences before, during and after the visit using online platforms (Kladou and Mavragani, 2015). Tripadvisor has emerged as a leading online social media platform to record the experiences of tourists during travel and is often used by others for advice (Dijkmans *et al.*, 2015; Cezar and Ögüt, 2016). Many tourists post reviews during or at the end of their travels. The basic motive of tourists sharing their reviews is to help others (O'Connor, 2010). With the inclusion of a badge system on Tripadvisor, there has been a sudden increase in the number of reviewers. It is also argued that the quality of reviews is higher if an incentive programme is in place (Liu *et al.*, 2018).

Research Methodology

Data collection

The purpose of the study is to understand the international tourists' culinary experiences and expectations with respect to Delhi street food. We chose online reviews from TripAdvisor as a data source for this study. Tripadvisor is a very popular travellers' review website. Hotels, restaurants, activities, places, beaches, flights and casinos are listed on Tripadvisor from across the globe. We chose New Delhi as a sample for the

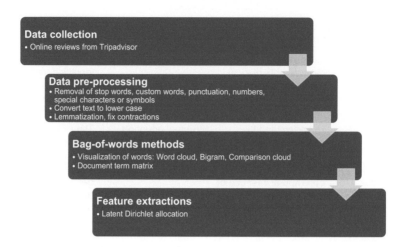

Fig. 7.1. Research process.
Source: Author's own work.

study because it is the capital of India and is in the top three states that attract foreign tourists. We collected 500 textual reviews from the food and drink category for further analysis.

Data pre-processing

Textual reviews are unstructured reviews written by tourists. To process for analysis, text data need to be cleaned. We used R programming for pre-processing and to analyse the data. Fig. 7.1 shows the text pre-processing steps, which include removal of special characters, numbers and punctuation. In text data, some words like 'the', 'is' and 'and' repeat frequently. We removed stop words and developed the custom word library to remove city names, people's names etc. The next step was converting text into lower case. Finally, we lemmatized the words into their root form (e.g. 'satisfied' converts to 'satisfaction').

Data analysis: bag-of-words method, and Latent Dirichlet allocation

The analysis comprised two parts: exploratory data analysis, and feature extraction.

Exploratory data analysis

Exploratory data analysis was used to calculate the technical features of the reviews (e.g. polarity score, word length, average contributions by tourists and number of reviews).

Feature extraction

To extract the features, N-gram analysis was computed. N-gram analysis computes the repeated phrases in text data (e.g. food tour, tasty food, gluten free). We set $N=2$ to compute bigram analysis. Dimensions were computed based on associated words. The first and third author was computed based on bigram results.

Results

Table 7.2 displays the descriptive statistics along with technical features of the reviews. A total of 443 reviews were collected. Of the reviews, 60% belonged to international tourists, 37% to others, 2% were written by Indian tourists. International tourists' average contribution was 55, whereas Indian tourists' contribution was 9 and others 6. The average helpful votes received by international tourists was 17; 4 votes for others, and for Indian reviewers it was 2.3.

Table 7.2. Descriptive statistics.

Type	Word length	Contribution	Helpful votes	Number of reviews
International tourists	125.272 (88.196)	55.325 (174.807)	17.751 (41.035)	265 (59.82)
Indian tourists	124.385 (92.430)	9.000 (11.372)	2.308 (3.660)	13 (2.93)
Others	98.303 (73.668)	6.182 (26.486)	3.927 (12.380)	165 (37.24)
Total	115.2 (83.937)	35.661 (138.019)	12.148 (33.277)	443

Table 7.3. Dimension extraction.

Dimension	Terms	Frequency
Food and local tour	food_tour, tour_guide, amaze_tour, local_tour, fun_tour, awesome_tour, lunch_tour, dinner_tour, heritage_tour	726
Guide behaviour	excellent_guide, tour_guide, amaze_guide, heritage_walk	171
Memorable food experience	delicious_food, amaze_food, love_food, lot_fun, enjoy_food, wonderful_expe, excellent_food, fantastic_food	170
Food quality	clean, gluten_free, safe_eat, smell_good, taste_good	164
Recommendation	highly_recommend, recommend_tour, strongly_recom, definite	144
Service quality	culture_food, history_culture, food_culture, friendly_speak, food_vendors, street_vendor	81
Education	food_learn, cook_class, learn_lot	76

Feature extraction

Table 7.3 shows the extracted features along with terms associated with them. With the help of previous literature and industry experts, the authors developed the seven dimensions that are experienced by international tourists concerning local street food. The authors considered the following while developing dimensions:

- The key terms for dimension 1 are *food_tour, tour_guide, local_tour, fun_tour*. This dimension is named as 'Food and local tour'.
- The key terms for dimension 2 are *excellent_guide, tour_guide, amazing_guide*. This dimension is named as 'Guide behaviour'.
- Dimension 3 is associated with terms such as *delicious_food, amaze_food, love_food, lot_fun,*

enjoy_food, and named as 'Memorable food experience'.

- Terms in dimension 4 include *clean, gluten_free, safe_eat, smell_good, taste_good*. This dimension is interpreted as 'Food quality'.
- Dimension 5 is predominantly associated with the terms *highly_recommend, recommended_tour, strongly_recommend, definite*, which can be interpreted as 'recommendation' or 'positive word-of-mouth'.
- The main terms associated with dimension 6 are *culture_food, history_culture, food_culture, friendly_speak, and street_vendor*, which can be interpreted as 'Service quality'.
- The last dimension's associated terms are *food_learn, cook_class, and learn_lot*, which can be named as 'Education'.

Discussion and Conclusion

This study examined the indicators of international tourists' experience of local street food in New Delhi. Food plays a very important role in the tourism industry. With the growth of the internet, many destinations are promoting street food to attract international and domestic tourists. By using social media platforms (e.g. YouTube, Instagram, Twitter and Facebook), local street vendors are promoting their unique foods (Fusté-Forné, 2020). For some tourists, food becomes the primary motive to travel to different destinations (Cleave, 2020). The study identified seven indicators that are experienced by tourists. These dimensions are: food and local tours, guide behaviour, memorable food experience, food quality, recommendations or positive word-of-mouth, service quality, and education or learning.

Food and local tours: Tourists mentioned their food tour and local tour experience. International tourists visit local food vendors to experience the local food offered by them.

Guide behaviour: Tourists mentioned guide behaviour. Due to the language barrier and to learn about the unique food offered by a destination, tourists depend on a guide, whereas the guide acts as a mediator between the vendor and the tourists. The guide explains the uniqueness of the food, the ingredients of the dishes and the history of the place very clearly. The role of the guide is very important to create a unique and memorable experience for tourists (Seyitoğlu, 2020).

Memorable food experience: Memorable food experiences create revisit intention and a positive image for a destination. Memorable experience plays an important role in tourist behaviour. Studies found that, after completion of the tour, tourists rethink or eat the food they tasted at the destination (Ji *et al.*, 2016). The purchasing and eating patterns may change after visiting the destination (Kim *et al.*, 2019).

Food quality: Tourists are concerned about safety and hygiene. Of utmost importance are ingredients used and cleanliness of the environment (Okumus *et al.*, 2018).

Recommendations or postive word-of-mouth: Satisfied tourists recommend the destination in many ways. Tourists write about their experience on third-party review websites, on social media and in blogs. Tourists share positive or negative experiences with their friends and family on social media (Oliveira *et al.*, 2020). Positive reviews improve sales which improve revenue for the service provider (Ye *et al.*, 2009). Negative reviews may damage the reputation of the service provider (Sparks and Browning, 2010).

Service quality: The behaviour of the guide and the service from vendors were important in creating positive impressions.

Education or learning: Tourists show interest in learning about food preparation methods. Some tourists may attend cooking classes offered by vendors (Piramanayagam and Seal, 2021).

Practical implications

Street food directly or indirectly provides employment opportunities for local people, which impacts their economy and improves their living standards. Food vendors and local destination providers need to understand the expectations and experiences of the international tourist. Results reveal very interesting facts. Tourists were very keen to learn about cooking processes, methods and ingredients used to prepare food, history and culture of a destination, and about vendors. Guides play an important role in accommodating international tourists. Street vendors should maintain hygiene and cleanliness standards to attract tourists. Positive experiences lead to positive word-of-mouth. Service providers should use social media to promote their street food offerings.

Limitations

This study has a few limitations. First, the results are based on a limited sample from New Delhi. The results may not be generalizable due to cultural issues. Second, we used basic text mining analysis (e.g. N-gram); future studies could use advanced text mining techniques (e.g. Latent Dirichlet allocation, latent semantic analysis) to get automated dimensions extracted using machine learning algorithms. Third, the sample contained positive reviews only; future studies could collect positive and negative results and compare the dimensions. Fourth, we applied unsupervised text mining techniques; further studies could focus on predictive techniques to check the impact of reviews on street food vendors' sales performance. Fifth, future studies could implement the Pine and Gilmore experience economy model using netnography.

References

Agyeiwaah, E., Otoo, F.E., Suntikul, W. and Huang, W.J. (2019) Understanding culinary tourist motivation, experience, satisfaction, and loyalty using a structural approach. *Journal of Travel & Tourism Marketing* 36(3), 295–313.

Andersson, T.D., Mossberg, L. and Therkelsen, A. (2017) Food and tourism synergies: Perspectives on consumption, production and destination development. *Scandinavian Journal of Hospitality and Tourism* 17(1), 1–8.

Aswani, R., Kar, A.K., Ilavarasan, P.V. and Dwivedi, Y.K. (2018) Search engine marketing is not all gold: insights from Twitter and SEO clerks. *International Journal of Information Management* 38(1), 107–116. DOI: 10.1016/j.ijinfomgt.2017.07.005.

Brown, M.D., Var, T. and Lee, S. (2002) Messina Hof Wine and Jazz Festival: an economic impact analysis. *Tourism Economics* 8(3), 273–279. DOI: 10.5367/000000002101298115.

Cezar, A. and Ögüt, H. (2016) Analyzing conversion rates in online hotel booking: the role of customer reviews, recommendations and rank order in search listings. *International Journal of Contemporary Hospitality Management* 28(2), 286–304.

Chang, R.C. and Mak, A.H. (2018) Understanding gastronomic image from tourists' perspective: A repertory grid approach. *Tourism Management* 68, 89–100. DOI: 10.1016/j.tourman.2018.03.004.

Cheung, S. (2009) Gastronomy and tourism: a case study of gourmet country-style cuisine in Hong Kong. In: Winter, T., Teo, P. and Chang, T.C. (eds) *Asia On Tour: Exploring the Rise of Asian Tourism*. Routledge Press, London, pp. 264–273. DOI: 10.4324/9780203891803.

Choe, J. and Kim, S. (2019) Development and validation of a multidimensional tourist's local food consumption value (TLFCV) scale. *International Journal of Hospitality Management* 77, 245–259. DOI: 10.1016/j.ijhm.2018.07.004.

Chuang, T.C., Liu, J.S., Lu, L.Y., Tseng, F.-M., Lee, Y. *et al.* (2017) The main paths of eTourism: trends of managing tourism through Internet. *Asia Pacific Journal of Tourism Research* 22(2), 213–231. DOI: 10.1080/10941665.2016.1220963.

Cleave, P. (2020) Food as a leisure pursuit, a United Kingdom perspective. *Annals of Leisure Research* 23(4), 474–491. DOI: 10.1080/11745398.2019.1613669.

Cohen, S.A., Prayag, G. and Moital, M. (2014) Consumer behaviour in tourism: concepts influences and opportunities. *Current Issues in Tourism* 17(10), 872–909. DOI: 10.1080/13683500.2013.850064.

Correia, A., Kim, S. and Kozak, M. (2020) Gastronomy experiential traits and their effects on intentions for recommendation: A fuzzy set approach. *International Journal of Tourism Research* 22(3), 351–363. DOI: 10.1002/jtr.2340.

Dijkmans, C., Kerkhof, P. and Beukeboom, C.J. (2015) A stage to engage: social media use and corporate reputation. *Tourism Management* 47, 58–67. DOI: 10.1016/j.tourman.2014.09.005.

Duarte Alonso, A. (2010) Olives, hospitality and tourism: a western Australian perspective. *British Food Journal* 112(1), 55–68. DOI: 10.1108/00070701011011209.

Ellis, A., Park, E., Kim, S. and Yeoman, I. (2018) What is food tourism? *Tourism Management* 68(October), 250–263. DOI: 10.1016/j.tourman.2018.03.025.

Fields, K. (2002) Demand for the gastronomy tourism product: motivational factors. In: Hjalager, A.M. and Richards, G. (eds) *Tourism and Gastronomy*. Routledge, London and New York, pp. 36–50.

Filieri, R., Alguezaui, S. and McLeay, F. (2015) Why do travelers trust TripAdvisor? Antecedents of trust towards consumer-generated media and its influence on recommendation adoption and word of mouth. *Tourism Management* 51, 174–185. DOI: 10.1016/j.tourman.2015.05.007.

Fusté-Forné, F. (2020) Savouring place: Cheese as a food tourism destination landmark. *Journal of Place Management and Development* 13, 177–194. DOI: 10.1108/JPMD-07-2019-0065.

Goolaup, S. and Mossberg, L. (2017) Exploring the concept of extraordinary related to food tourists' nature-based experience. *Scandinavian Journal of Hospitality and Tourism* 17(1), 27–43. DOI: 10.1080/15022250.2016.1218150.

Guo, Y., Barnes, S.J. and Jia, Q. (2017) Mining meaning from online ratings and reviews: tourist satisfaction analysis using latent dirichlet allocation. *Tourism Management* 59, 467–483. DOI: 10.1016/j.tourman.2016.09.009.

Hendijani, R.B. (2016) Effect of food experience on tourist satisfaction: the case of Indonesia. *International Journal of Culture, Tourism and Hospitality Research* 10(3), 272–282. DOI: 10.1108/IJCTHR-04-2015-0030.

Hernández, J.M., Kirilenko, A.P. and Stepchenkova, S. (2018) Network approach to tourist segmentation via user generated content. *Annals of Tourism Research* 73, 35–47. DOI: 10.1016/j.annals.2018.09.002.

Hindley, A. and Wall, T. (2018) *Markets, Festivals and Shows: Sustainable Approaches to Gastronomic Tourism through Collaboration*. Routledge.

Holmberg, C., Chaplin, J.E., Hillman, T. and Berg, C. (2016) Adolescents' presentation of food in social media: an explorative study. *Appetite* 99(April), 121–129. DOI: 10.1016/j.appet.2016.01.009.

Horng, J.S. and Tsai, C.T. (2012) Culinary tourism strategic development: an Asia-Pacific perspective. *International Journal of Tourism Research* 14(1), 40–55. DOI: 10.1002/jtr.834.

Hwang, J., Kim, S.S., Choe, J.Y.J. and Chung, C.H. (2018) Exploration of the successful glocalization of ethnic food: a case of Korean food. *International Journal of Contemporary Hospitality Management* 30(12), 3656–3676. DOI: 10.1108/IJCHM-07-2017-0452.

Ji, M., Wong, I.A., Eves, A. and Scarles, C. (2016) Food-related personality traits and the moderating role of novelty-seeking in food satisfaction and travel outcomes. *Tourism Management* 57, 387–396.

Kim, S., Choe, J. and Lee, S. (2018) Effects of food value video clips on increasing the demand for food tourism: Generation Y versus non-Generation Y. *Journal of Travel & Tourism Marketing* 35(3), 377–393.

Kim, S., Chen, J., Cheng, T., Gindulyte, A., He, J, *et al.* (2019) PubChem 2019 update: improved access to chemical data. *Nucleic Acids Research* 47(D1), D1102–D1109.

Kladou, S. and Mavragani, E. (2015) Assessing destination image: an online marketing approach and the case of TripAdvisor. *Journal of Destination Marketing & Management* 4(3), 187–193. DOI: 10.1016/j.jdmm.2015.04.003.

Lee, K.H., Packer, J. and Scott, N. (2015) Travel lifestyle preferences and destination activity choices of slow food members and non-members. *Tourism Management* 46, 1–10. DOI: 10.1016/j.tourman.2014.05.008.

Leung, D., Law, R., van Hoof, H. and Buhalis, D. (2013) Social media in tourism and hospitality: a literature review. *Journal of Travel & Tourism Marketing* 30(1–2), 3–22. DOI: 10.1080/10548408.2013.750919.

Liu, X., Schuckert, M. and Law, R. (2018) Utilitarianism and knowledge growth during status seeking: evidence from text mining of online reviews. *Tourism Management* 66, 38–46. DOI: 10.1016/j.tourman.2017.11.005.

Moutinho, L. (1987) Consumer behaviour in tourism. *European Journal of Marketing* 21(10), 5–44. DOI: 10.1108/EUM0000000004718.

Nair, B.B. (2017) The politics of tourism representations: discourse analysis of British travel brochures about incredible India. *Journal of Advanced Research in Social Sciences and Humanities* 2(4), 230–236. DOI: 10.26500/JARSSH-02-2017-0401.

O'Connor, P. (2010) Managing a hotel's image on Tripadvisor. *Journal of Hospitality Marketing & Management* 19(7), 754–772. DOI: 10.1080/19368623.2010.508007.

Okumus, B., Okumus, F. and McKercher, B. (2007) Incorporating local and international cuisines in the marketing of tourism destinations: the cases of Hong Kong and Turkey. *Tourism Management* 28(1), 253–261. DOI: 10.1016/j.tourman.2005.12.020.

Okumus, B., Ali, F., Bilgihan, A. and Ozturk, A.B. (2018) Psychological factors influencing customers' acceptance of smartphone diet apps when ordering food at restaurants. *International Journal of Hospitality Management* 72, 67–77. DOI: 10.1016/j.ijhm.2018.01.001.

Oliveira, B.S., Tricárico, L.T., Sohn, A.P.L. and Pontes, N. (2020) The culinary intangible cultural heritage of UNESCO: A review of journal articles in EBSCO platform. *Journal of Culinary Science & Technology* 18(2), 138–156.

Piramanayagam, S. and Seal, P.P. (2021) Employers' attitudes and hiring intentions towards persons with disabilities in hotels in India. *Disability, CBR and Inclusive Development*. Available at: https://papers.ssrn.com/sol3/papers.cfm?abstract_id=3866663

Rodrigues, M.D.O.B. (2020) *The impact of virtual reality in the motion picture industry regarding brand coolness, emotional responses, and WOM.* Doctoral dissertation. Instituto Universitario de Lisboa. Available at: https://repositorio.iscte-iul.pt/bitstream/10071/21900/1/master_mariana_berga_rodrigues.pdf

Schuckert, M., Liu, X.W. and Law, R. (2015) Hospitality and tourism online reviews: recent trends and future directions. *Journal of Travel & Tourism Marketing* 32, 608–621. DOI: 10.1080/10548408.2014.933154.

Seaman, C., Quinn, M.B., Björk, P. and Kauppinen-Räisänen, H. (2014) Culinary-gastronomic tourism – a search for local food experiences. *Nutrition & Food Science* 44(4).

Seyitoğlu, F. (2020) Tourists' perceptions of the tour guides: The case of gastronomic tours in Istanbul. *Anatolia* 31(3), 393–405.

Silkes, C.A., Cai, L.A. and Lehto, X.Y. (2013) Marketing to the culinary tourist. *Journal of Travel & Tourism Marketing* 30(4), 335–349. DOI: 10.1080/10548408.2013.784151.

Simeon, M.I., Buonincontri, P., Cinquegrani, F. and Martone, A. (2017) Exploring tourists' cultural experiences in Naples through online reviews. *Journal of Hospitality and Tourism Technology* 8(2), 220–238. DOI: 10.1108/JHTT-10-2016-0067.

Sparks, B., Bowen, J. and Klag, S. (2003) Restaurants and the tourist market. *International Journal of Contemporary Hospitality Management* 15(1), 6–13. DOI: 10.1108/09596110310458936.

Sparks, B.A. and Browning, V. (2010) Complaining in cyberspace: The motives and forms of hotel guests' complaints online. *Journal of Hospitality Marketing & Management* 19(7), 797–818.

Stone, M.J., Migacz, S. and Sthapit, E. (2022) Connections between culinary tourism experiences and memory. *Journal of Hospitality & Tourism Research* 46(4), 797–807.

Stone, M.J., Soulard, J., Migacz, S. and Wolf, E. (2018) Elements of memorable food, drink, and culinary tourism experiences. *Journal of Travel Research* 57(8), 1121–1132. DOI: 10.1177/0047287517729758.

Suntikul, W. (2019) Gastrodiplomacy in tourism. *Current Issues in Tourism* 22(9), 1076–1094. DOI: 10.1080/13683500.2017.1363723.

Tamrakar, C., Pyo, T.H. and Gruca, T. (2018) Social media sentiment and firm value. Available at: https://bit.ly/32oF6Pl (accessed 27 December 2022)

Tsai, C.T. (2016) Memorable tourist experiences and place attachment when consuming local food. *International Journal of Tourism Research* 18(6), 536–548. DOI: 10.1002/jtr.2070.

Tsai, C.T. and Wang, Y.C. (2017) Experiential value in branding food tourism. *Journal of Destination Marketing & Management* 6(1), 56–65. DOI: 10.1016/j.jdmm.2016.02.003.

Vengesayi, S., Mavondo, F.T. and Reisinger, Y. (2009) Tourism destination attractiveness: attractions, facilities, and people as predictors. *Tourism Analysis* 14(5), 621–636. DOI: 10.3727/108354209X12597959359211.

Wang, X. (2011) Model for tourism management with 2-tuple linguistic information. *Advances in Information Sciences and Service Sciences* 3(4), 34–39. DOI: 10.4156/aiss.vol3.issue4.5.

Ye, Q., Law, R. and Gu, B. (2009) The impact of online user reviews on hotel room sales. *International Journal of Hospitality Management* 28(1), 180–182. DOI: 10.1016/j.ijhm.2008.06.011.

8 A Comparative Study of Waste Management Practices in Pre-COVID and During-COVID Scenarios: An Overview of the Hotel Industry

Sonali Chhetri[1]* and Amit Kumar[2]

[1]*Department of Hospitality Management, CT University, Ludhiana, Punjab, India;*
[2]*School of Hotel Management, Airlines and Tourism, CT University, Ludhiana, Punjab, India*

Abstract

The COVID-19 pandemic has been challenging for the hotel industry, with rooms being converted into quarantine centres and leading to an increase in waste volume and composition. With frequent lockdowns and stringent guidelines by governments on social distancing, 60% of hotels converted 10% of their rooms into quarantine facilities, which drastically changed the composition of hotel waste (JLL, 2020). This waste may lead to environmental degradation if handled inappropriately. The primary objective of this study is to identify, compare and highlight the challenges faced in waste management practices in two different circumstances, namely pre-COVID and during-COVID, in the hotel industry. Data were collected using a structured questionnaire put to hoteliers in selected hotels in India. A total of 61 responses were recorded out of 100 respondents. Descriptive analysis indicated new practices in hotel housekeeping such as use of single-use PPE kits, arrangement of separate zones for disposing of medical waste and digitalization of services. Another interesting finding of the research is the aggravation of single-use plastic in the form of disposable crockery, cutlery and packaging of PPE kits. Lastly, the study showed an increase in operational costs and highlighted innovative procedures in existing waste management disposal practices and suggested new practices that will be of great significance for dealing with similar episodes in the future.

Introduction

India is the most desired tourist destination in the world for its exquisitely rich culture, heritage and geographical diversity, as projected by the World Travel and Tourism Council ((WTTC, 2019). In order to intensify travel and tourism, the government of India has declared 17 iconic Indian tourist sites as world-class destinations (Union Budget 2019–20, Govt of India) (Indian brand equity foundation, 2020) brand equity foundation, 2020). Tourism contributes strongly to local financial health by generating employment but it also adversely impacts the environment (Competitiveness-index, 2019). It is responsible for generating large volumes of waste due to economic development, urbanization and commercial activity in the cities of India. India produces 62 million tonnes of waste annually,

*Corresponding author: sonalitiwari0302@gmail.com

© CAB International 2023. *Technology and Social Transformations in Hospitality, Tourism and Gastronomy: South Asia Perspectives* (eds S. Sharma and S. Bhartiya)
DOI: 10.1079/9781800621244.0008

out of which tourism and hotels contribute 30% (Goodtourismblog, 2019). As (Census of India, 2011) reports, total waste generated in Mumbai was 6500 tonnes per day. New Delhi produced 5800 tonnes, Chennai produced 4500 tonnes and Hyderabad produced 4200 tonnes, which shows that cities of India are highly polluting and that the implementation of sustainable waste management practices in every operation is very important.

Undoubtedly, the hotel industry has been facing pressure from the government to incorporate sustainable waste management practices to minimize the negative impact on the environment (Erdogan and Baris, 2007). Earlier reviews on waste reveal that it is generated by human group activities. When the population was smaller and availability of land was easier, waste disposal was not a major concern; it would biodegrade naturally in open spaces (Chandler et al., 1997). Waste generation increased during the 16th century when people started travelling due to the Industrial Revolution, leading to a change in waste composition with the introduction of metals and plastics. This deviation led to indiscriminate littering and uncontrolled dumping in open spaces, posing a risk to human health (Wilson, 2007). Consequently, policies on safeguarding human health began during the 19th century with public officials focusing primarily on systematic waste disposal (Shanklin et al., 1991; Tchobanoglous et al., 1993). Today, due to rapid urbanization and development, waste management has become the subject of research study. Similarly, with the intensive growth of the hotel industry over the past decade, hotels remain the primary consumers of natural resources and contribute enormously to waste volume. The environmental impact created by hotels can be seen in excessive consumption of non-durable products and increased carbon footprint, leading to air pollution (APAT, 2002; Kumar, 2005). When COVID-19 gripped the world, single-use plastic was recommended in the hotel industry to protect people from virus transmission (National Library of Medicine, 2021). However, with stringent policies and guidelines from government on sanitation and hygiene, the hotel industry has been effectively implementing waste management practices focusing on reusing, reducing and recycling in its daily operations. The Marriott and IHG chains

of hotels, which own over 7000 and 5600 hotels, respectively, areound the globe, with brand names such as Le Meridian, Renaissance, Crowne Plaza and Holiday Inn, declared they would stop using single-use plastic amenities and bottles by December 2020. Conversely, the COVID-19 pandemic has created a complete change, with many hotels using doll's house-sized toiletries and sanitizing wipes, after reopening, for guest safety (The Independent, 2019).

The World Health Organisation (WHO), (2020), declared a pandemic on 11 March 2020, after the geographical expansion of COVID-19. With frequent lockdowns and social distancing, 60% of hotels converted 10% of their rooms into quarantine facilities, which drastically changed the composition of hotel waste, (JLL, 2020). Wuhan in China generated 247 tonnes of medical waste per day, nearly six times more than before the pandemic, while the city has waste disposal capacity of only 50 tonnes per day (Singh et al., 2020). Likewise, during COVID-19, hotel waste included biomedical waste like PPE kits and plastics, separate from kitchen waste (The Indenpendent, 2020). The demand for single-use plastics has increased as most hotel guests perceived plastic-bottled water and packaged food to be more hygienic during the pandemic. In addition, it has reformed the frequency of cleaning and sanitization of various touch points and surfaces leading to a complete change in standard operating procedures. This study focuses on the comparative analysis of housekeeping practices towards waste management in pre-COVID and during-COVID scenarios.

Literature Review

Hoornweg and Bhada-Tata (2012) stated that, globally, 1.3 million tonnes (1.2 kg/capita/day) of waste are generated annually, and this is expected to increase by 2.2 billion tonnes by 2025. Amasuomo and Baird (2016) explained that solid waste, if left uncollected, leads to air pollution and blocking of drains and poses risks to human health.

The ACCOR hotel group has developed a programme called Planet 21, which frames sustainable strategies to reduce food waste and create a positive environment in the hotel industry (ACCOR, 2019). Dijkema *et al.* (2000) revealed in their review paper that an item may be waste to one individual but a resource to another. The owner labels it. They stated that policies can be effectively planned to prevent indiscriminate littering and disposal causing risk to human health. Gandhi *et al.* (2019) reported in their survey of Indian hotels that customers' eating habits, style of service and food portions are the primary reasons for generating food waste. The increase in food waste is also seen more during dinner (30%), as compared to breakfast (15%). Similarly, Okumus (2020) stated that poor menu planning, uncontrolled portion sizes and over-ordering are the most common reasons for food waste in hotels. Their findings also stated that customers' demand for expanded menus leads to food waste. Shamshiry *et al.* (2011) and Abd Manaf *et al.* (2009) established that government needs to develop strategies and technological innovations to improve waste management practices in the organizations to reduce operational costs and negative impacts on society.

A report by the Ministry of Environment, Forest and Climate Change (2015) introduced waste management and handling rules , and it is responsible for handling waste. It states that biomedical and general waste should be disposed of separately at source. The local municipal authorities are responsible for implementing and developing infrastructure for collecting, storing, segregating, transporting, processing and disposing of waste. Kasemsap (2017) and Kumar *et al.* (2017) indicated that it is essential to change the attitudes of people towards managing waste in their organization and suggested segregating waste at source and developing effective and sustainable waste management practices. Radwan *et al.* (2012) confirmed that, compared to large hotels, small hotels are highly dependent on landfill for waste disposal; they lack awareness on sustainable waste management practices and need to be educated. Francis *et al.* (2013) concluded that it is essential for organizations to collect and segregate waste at source and apply the concept of recycling to reduce the volume and characteristics of waste. Wolfe and Shanklin (2001) mentioned that the hotel industry should emphasize the concept of recycling, develop comprehensive employee

training programmes and focus on minimizing waste. Omidiani and Hashemi Hezaveh (2016) revealed that most waste produced in the hotel industry is recyclable and can generate revenue for the organization. Pham Phu *et al.* (2018) pointed out that the larger the size and higher the category of hotel, the higher is the waste generation rate, with waste composition identified primarily as biodegradable and recyclable. The study also revealed higher-scale hotels are conscious of waste management practices. Goh *et al.* (2017) concluded that it is essential for the hospitality industry to engage young employees to educate and train, as they acknowledge the consequences of waste and are flexible and ready for change. Amasuomo and Baird (2016) and Singh *et al.* (2020) mentioned that developing countries should work on creating comprehensive waste disposal methods like on-site emergency disposal with the minimum number of workers on site to avoid the spread of infection.

The WHO (2020) specified a temporary relaxation of production and use of single-use plastic in the COVID-19 pandemic as plastic packaging for gloves, masks, PPE kits and bio-waste bags increased to meet global demand. Sharma *et al.* (2020) indicated that active cooperation and participation of consumers in handling waste are considered an effective way to control the negative impacts of waste during the pandemic. Silva *et al.* (2020) revealed that the sudden demand for plastic-packaged products like gloves, masks, water bottles and other basic amenities has increased significantly during the pandemic, thus necessitating an urgent effort to introduce vigorous policies for sustainable solutions. Sarkodie and Owusu (2021) concluded that increased consumption and production of single-use products have increased during the pandemic and this emphasizes the need for urgent and effective waste management practices.

The Objectives of the Study

The objectives of this study are:

1. to identify the hotel waste management practices in pre- and during-COVID scenarios

2. to compare waste management practices in pre- and during-COVID scenarios; and
3. to identify challenges and suggest measures for improving waste management practices post-COVID-19.

Research Methodology

Sampling and data collection

The data for the research study were collected from the hotel employees and their employers. A survey was conducted using a structured questionnaire distributed to respondents through an online platform. The questionnaire was framed with 'closed' questions and filled in by the respondents during the period January–March 2021. The questionnaire was divided into three sections. The first section concerned the demographic profile of the respondent. The second section consisted of numerous closed questions on waste management practices pre-COVID and during-COVID in the hotel industry. The third section consisted of questions on the challenges faced while handling waste and suggested measures to improve waste management services post-COVID-19. The secondary sources of information were derived from a combination of electronic and printed materials such as books, research papers and journals. The primary source data was the structured questionnaires collected from hoteliers.

Analysis and Findings

Demographic characteristics of respondents

To accomplish the above-mentioned objectives, 61 out of 100 respondents filled in the questionnaire. The gender distribution showed that the majority of the respondents were male (78.7%). The survey statistics indicated that 82% of the respondents were from star-category hotels and 16.4% were from non-star properties; 26.2% respondents were from the housekeeping department, 9.8% from the food production department. Front office and food and beverage departments showed an identical response of 19.7%. The analysis also included the job positions of the hotel personnel with 41% as heads of departments, 13.1% as supervisors, 11.5% as hotel proprietors and 9.8% as general managers (Table 8.1).

Identification of waste management practices pre-COVID and during-COVID in the hotel industry

From the previous literature review it has been observed that there were numerous practices concerning waste management in the hotel industry during the pre-COVID scenario. The most prominent practices include provision of masks and gloves, use of colour-coded dustbins,

Table 8.1. Demographic characteristics of respondents.

Gender	Respondents (%)	Hotel category	Respondents (%)
Male	78.7	Star-category hotels	82
Female	21.3	Non-star category	16.4
		Heritage hotels	1.6
		Supplementary units	Nil
Hotel Departments	**Respondents (%)**	**Job position**	**Respondents (%)**
Housekeeping	26.2	Department heads	41
Other	24.6	Others	24.6
Food and beverage	19.7	Supervisors	13.1
Front office	19.7	Proprietors	11.5
Food production	9.8	General managers	9.8

Source: Author's own work.

regular training of hotel employees, segregation of wet and dry waste at source, and donating leftover food to NGOs as part of corporate social responsibility. As a result of government policies, new practices like segregation of medical waste and general waste, use of biodegradable bags for waste disposal, introduction of a COVID committee for supervising practices, government-approved vendors for garbage collection, and digitalization of menu cards were incorporated during the operation. The study clearly indicates some new practices in force during the pandemic.

Comparison of waste management practices in pre-COVID and during-COVID scenarios

A comparison of waste management practices was conducted by the researcher in pre-COVID and during-COVID hotel scenarios (Table 8.2). The result of the study indicated that 42.6% of the surveyed hotels received medical waste like gloves and masks in the pre-COVID period as these protective kits were provided to the

Table 8.2. Waste management practices in pre- and during-COVID scenarios in hotels.

Waste management practices in hotels	Pre-COVID (%)	During COVID (%)	Both cases (%)	Does not implement (%)
Does the hotel receive medical waste like gloves and masks in the garbage?	42.6	44.2	1.6	11.4
Do you segregate medical waste like gloves and masks from general waste on a daily basis?	8.1	31.1	45.9	14.7
Do you provide PPE kits, gloves and masks to sanitary workers in your hotel?	8.1	60.6	26.2	4.9
Do you use colour-coded dustbins for disposing of different types of waste?	11.4	18	67.2	3.2
Do you follow any standard guidelines for disposing of different types of waste?	13.1	8.1	75.4	3.2
Do you have a special committee to handle waste management in your hotel?	11.4	13.1	63.9	11.4
Do you conduct regular training to sanitary workers on waste management?	9.8	18	63.9	8.1
Do you have government-approved vendors to collect bio-waste and general waste?	9.8	11.4	73.7	4.9
Do you segregate different types of hotel waste at source?	6.5	9.8	77	6.5
Do you dispose of your general waste and medical waste in biodegradable bags?	4.9	16.3	70.4	8.1
Does your hotel restaurant provide a digital menu to the guests?	3.2	42	39.3	14.7
Does the hotel donate leftover food to NGOs as part of CSR activity?	11.4	14.7	36	42.6

Source: Author's own work.

sanitation workers and housekeepers as part of the hotels' safety practices; 1.6% of hotels received the same amount of medical waste in both cases, and 44.2% observed an increase during the COVID pandemic. A small percentage of hotels (8.1%) segregated medical waste and general waste pre-COVID, whereas 31.1% hotels started to segregate on a daily basis during COVID; and 45.9% of hotels followed this practice in both scenarios. Provision of PPE kits to sanitary workers during COVID was high at 60.6% as compared to pre-COVID (8.1%). Practices like use of colour-coded dustbins for disposing of different types of waste remained high, at 67.2%, in both scenarios but showed an increase during COVID, as only 11.4% of hotels had implemented this practice in the pre-COVID period.

The study revealed that 75.4% of hotels had standard guidelines for waste management in both the scenarios but formation of a special committee for handling waste was adopted by 13.1% of hotels during COVID as compared to 11.4% pre-COVID. However, in spite of stringent guidelines by WHO, 11.4% of hotels had not formed a committee, even after the outbreak of the pandemic. Similarly, 63.9% of hotels conducted regular training for sanitary workers in both cases but the percentage was almost doubled during COVID (18%) as compared to 9.8% pre-COVID. Another remarkable fact is that 77% of hotels segregated different types of waste at source pre- and during-COVID, and 9.8% of hotels started implementing this practice during COVID, with only 6.5% of hotels practising it before. Hence, the research gives evidence that, although most hotels practised proper steps on waste handling, the pandemic has prompted hotels to be more careful in managing their waste.

The findings of the study stated that hotels (73.7%) have government-approved vendors to collect waste; 9.8% had vendors pre-COVID whereas this increased to 11.4% during the COVID period due to awareness of the risk of infection. Earlier, about 4.9% of hotels disposed of medical and general waste in biodegradable bags, but due to the pandemic, 16.3% of hotels started using yellow coded bags. Similarly, the pandemic provoked 42% of hotels to adopt digitalization of the food menu to provide contactless service while only 3.2% hotels

followed this practice before the pandemic. 36% of hotels donated leftover food to NGOs in both scenarios, but with public health and safety taking centre-stage during the pandemic; this dropped to 14.7% during COVID. A majority of hotels (42.6%) did not donate leftover food at all as they were scared of food poisoning and contamination.

The questionnaire also showed an increase in the implementation of single-use plastics as most hotel guests perceived plastic-bottled water and packaged food to be more hygienic. This showed an increase in waste composition during the pandemic (75.4%). Secondly, with high use of gloves, face shields and masks, 80% of hotels have seen a change in the volume of waste during the COVID period (Fig. 8.1). Finally, the study also revealed that due to various guidelines and policies on the safeguarding of human health during the pandemic, 70.4% of the hotels have seen an increase in their operational costs.

Identification of challenges in the hotel industry during the pandemic

From the various surveyed hotels in India, the researchers identified numerous challenges faced by the hotel industry during the pandemic. The study revealed that though there were placement of colour-coded dustbins in public areas, many guests and staff did not use them effectively. Creation and maintenance of a separate disposal area for medical waste was a major challenge as most sanitary workers were unskilled and required frequent supervision. Disposal of sanitizer sachets, face masks, shields and gloves at source was a challenge initially as guests had a casual approach to these practices. Similarly segregation and storage of waste like masks was difficult in the main garbage area as there was risk of the spread of infection. It was difficult for hotels to train and change the mindset of staff towards new COVID practices in a short period of time. The vendors allocated by government for collecting medical waste did not arrive on a daily basis due to frequent lockdowns, making it necessary for hotels to hire freelance agencies. Other challenges included educating hotel guests to use customized bins for COVID waste and monitoring them on a frequent

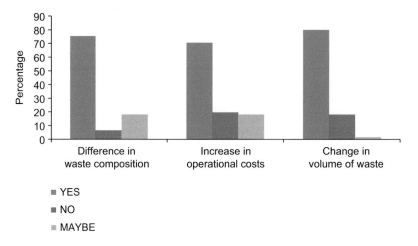

Fig. 8.1. Major changes in waste management during COVID.
Source: Author's own work.

basis. Many starred hotels, like ITC, introduced hygiene marshals, with hotel managers being trained to handle necessary COVID issues. It can be concluded that the provision of PPE to sanitary workers and an increase in operational costs are considered to be two of the major challenges, presently and in the future.

Suggested measures for improving waste management practices post-COVID-19

There were a few suggestions from respondents for improving waste management practices during and post-COVID. Suggestions included:

- frequent remedial training of hotel staff following guidelines shared by WHO and local government;
- continuous inspection to be done by floor supervisors for proper disposal of medical and general waste;
- more innovative practices on digitalization in all departments to be implemented in future to minimize human contact;
- use of PPE kits to be continued in future for sanitary workers to avoid risk of infection and to make it cost-effective for the hotel;
- more use of multilingual signage in public areas to educate guests about COVID guidelines;

- minimizing single-use plastic gradually and working on recyclable practices, as there has been an increase during the pandemic;
- government to offer subsidies to hotels for hygiene and sanitation since the pandemic has increased the operational costs of the hotel industry; and
- introduction of technology-based waste management equipment to minimize human contact.

Conclusion

Our findings clearly indicate that waste management practices were not new to the hotel industry before the pandemic but many new practices like maintenance of a separate area for disposing of medical waste and single-use PPE kits for sanitary workers have been implemented. Hotels have also followed guidelines shared by the Ministry of Tourism, the government of India, and the WHO on the infection-prevention programme for reopening hotels. The findings of the second objective stated that most of the hotels followed waste management practices pre-COVID and during COVID but showed that more hotels started to implement waste management practices rigorously during the pandemic with practices such as segregation of medical waste and general waste on a daily basis, use of disposable PPE kits, frequent training of staff on COVID guidelines and digitalization of services, though the donation of leftover food to NGOs showed a low response during the pandemic as it was percieved to hold a risk of spreading of contamination and infection.

The findings of the third objective expressed an increase in operational costs as one of the major perpetual challenges for the hotel industry and guests' casual approach towards COVID guidelines.

The respondents were aware of the spread of COVID-19 and recommended suggestions on improving hotel services and facilities. The suggestions included continuous training of staff on COVID guidelines and continuous inspection of the practices, as well as more innovative practices on digitalization in all departments to minimize human contact, use of PPE kits to be implemented on a daily basis, and introduction of technology-based waste management equipment to minimize human contact.

Limitation of the Study and Future Research

As this research was done during lockdown, the survey did not allow in-person contact and recording of resondents' opinions. Secondly, as most hotels were not open in March 2020, it was impossible for the questionnaire to be completed by hotel employees and employers, thus leading to a reduction in the number of responses. As the present research was conducted comparing waste management practices pre- and during-COVID, future studies could be conducted on the challenges for the hotel industry for waste management post-pandemic, or on customers' sentiments about patronizing hotels post-pandemic.

References

Abd Manaf, L., Samah, M.A.A. and Zukki, N.I.M. (2009) Municipal solid waste management in Malaysia: practices and challenges. *Waste Management (New York, N.Y.)* 29(11), 2902–2906. DOI: 10.1016/j.wasman.2008.07.015.

ACCOR (2019) Planet 21. Available at: https://www. accorhotels.com /sustainabledevelopment/index.shtml (accessed 6 January 2019).

Amasuomo, E. and Baird, J. (2016) The concept of waste and waste management. *Journal of Management and Sustainability* 6(4), 88. DOI: 10.5539/jms.v6n4p88.

Census of India (2011) Ministry of Home Affairs, Government of India, New Delhi, India. Available at: http ://census india.gov.in/ (accessed 27 June 2015).

Chandler, A.J., Eighmy, T.T., Hjelmar, O., Kosson, D.S., Sawell, S.E. *et al.* (1997) *Municipal Solid Waste Incinerator Residues*. Elsevier.

Competitiveness-index (2019). Available at: https://economictimes.indiatimes.com/industry/services/travel/india-moves-up-6-places-to-34th-rank-on-world-travel-tourism-competitiveness-index-wef-report/articleshow/70976484.cms?from=mdr (accessed 28 December 2022).

Dijkema, G.P.J., Reuter, M.A. and Verhoef, E.V. (2000) A new paradigm for waste management. *Waste Management* 20(8), 633–638. DOI: 10.1016/S0956-053X(00)00052-0.

Erdogan, N. and Baris, E. (2007) Environmental protection programs and conservation practices of hotels in Ankara, Turkey. *Tourism Management* 28(2), 604–614. DOI: 10.1016/j.tourman.2006.07.003.

Francis, R.C., Singh, L.P. and Prakash, E.V. (2013) Solid waste management and characteristics in Lucknow, Uttar Pradesh, India. *International Journal of Scientific & Engineering Research* 4, 11.

Gandhi, P., Kumar, S., Paritosh, K., Pareek, N. and Vivekanand, V. (2019) Hotel generated food waste and its biogas potential: a case study of Jaipur city, India. *Waste and Biomass Valorization* 10(6), 1459–1468. DOI: 10.1007/s12649-017-0153-1.

Goh, E., Muskat, B. and Tan, A.H.T. (2017) The nexus between sustainable practices in hotels and future Gen Y hospitality students' career path decisions. *Journal of Teaching in Travel & Tourism* 17(4), 237–253. DOI: 10.1080/15313220.2017.1362971.

Goodtourismblog (2019) Piling up India tourism waste management problem. Available at: https://goodtourismblog.com/2019/06/ (accessed 3 June 2019).

Hoornweg, D. and Bhada-Tata, P. (2012) What a waste: a global review of solid waste management. Available at: https://openknowledge.worldbank.org (accessed June 2021).

Indian brand equity foundation industry/tourism-hospitality-India (2020). Available at: https://www.ibef.org (accessed 28 December 2022).

Italian Agency for Environmental Protection and Technical Services (APAT) (2002). Available at: www.apat .gov.it/ certificazioni/site/_contentfiles/3rdActivityReport

JLL (2020) Impact of COVID-19 on the indian hospitality industry. Available at: https://www.jll.co.in/en/ trends-and-insights/research/hotel operatorssurvey (accessed 9 July 2020).

Kasemsap, K. (2017) Environmental management and waste management: principles and applications. In: *Ethics and Sustainability in Global Supply Chain Management*. IGI Global, pp. 26–49.

Kumar, S. (2005) Resource use and waste management in Vietnam hotel industry. *Journal of Cleaner Production* 13(2), 109–116. DOI: 10.1016/j.jclepro.2003.12.014.

Kumar, S., Smith, S.R., Fowler, G., Velis, C., Kumar, S.J. *et al.* (2017) Challenges and opportunities associated with waste management in India. *Royal Society Open Science* 4(3), 160764. DOI: 10.1098/rsos.160764.

Ministry of Environment, Forest and Climate Change (2015). Available at: https://tnpcb.gov.in/pdf_2019/SWM_Rules_2016 (accessed April 2016).

National Library of Medicine (2021) Plastic and its consequences during the Covid-19 pandemic. Available at: https://www.ncbi.nlm.nih.gov (accessed 21 July 2021). DOI: 10.1007/s11356-021-15425-w.

Okumus, B. (2020) How do hotels manage food waste? Evidence from hotels in Orlando, Florida. *Journal of Hospitality Marketing & Management* 29(3), 291–309. DOI: 10.1080/19368623.2019.1618775.

Omidiani, A. and Hashemi Hezaveh, S. (2016) Waste management in hotel industry in India: a review. *International Journal of Scientific and Research Publications* 6(9), 670–680.

Pham Phu, S.T., Hoang, M.G. and Fujiwara, T. (2018) Analyzing solid waste management practices for the hotel industry. *Global Journal of Environmental Science and Management* 4(1), 19–30.

Radwan, H.R.I., Jones, E. and Minoli, D. (2012) Solid waste management in small hotels: a comparison of green and non-green small hotels in Wales. *Journal of Sustainable Tourism* 20(4), 533–550. DOI: 10.1080/09669582.2011.621539.

Sarkodie, S.A. and Owusu, P.A. (2021) Impact of COVID-19 pandemic on waste management. *Environment, Development and Sustainability* 1–10.

Shamshiry, E., Nadi, B., Mokhtar, M., Komoo, I., Hashim, H. *et al.* (2011) Integrated models for solid waste management in tourism regions: Langkawi Island, Malaysia. *Journal of Environmental and Public Health* 2011, 709549. DOI: 10.1155/2011/709549.

Shanklin, C.W., Petrillose, M.J. and Pettay, A. (1991) Solid waste management practices in selected hotel chains and individual properties. *Hospitality Research Journal* 15(1), 59–74. DOI: 10.1177/109634809101500106.

Sharma, H.B., Vanapalli, K.R., Cheela, V.S., Ranjan, V.P., Jaglan, A.K. *et al.* (2020) Challenges, opportunities, and innovations for effective solid waste management during and post COVID-19 pandemic. *Resources, Conservation, and Recycling* 162, 105052. DOI: 10.1016/j.resconrec.2020.105052.

Silva, A.L.P., Prata, J.C., Walker, T.R., Campos, D., Duarte, A.C. *et al.* (2020) Rethinking and optimising plastic waste management under COVID-19 pandemic: policy solutions based on redesign and reduction of single-use plastics and personal protective equipment. *The Science of the Total Environment* 742, 140565. DOI: 10.1016/j.scitotenv.2020.140565.

Singh, N., Tang, Y. and Ogunseitan, O.A. (2020) Environmentally sustainable management of used personal protective equipment. *Environmental Science & Technology* 54(14), 8500–8502. DOI: 10.1021/acs.est.0c03022.

Tchobanoglous, G., Theisen, H. and Vigil, S. (1993) *Integrated Solid Waste Management: Engineering Principles and Management Lssues*. McGraw-Hill.

The Independent (2019) Marriott to get rid of small plastic toiletries in all its hotels by next year. Available at: https://www.independent.co.uk/travel/news-and-advice/marriott-international-hotels-single-use -plastic-amenities-2020-a9082391.html (accessed August 2019).

The Indenpendent (2020) How do we tackle the rising tide of pandemic-driven plastic waste? Available at: https://www.independent.co.uk/climate-change/news/plastic-pollution-single-use-waste-climate-coronavirus-a9567456.html (accessed December 2020).

Wilson, D.C. (2007) Development drivers for waste management. *Waste Management & Research* 25(3), 198–207. DOI: 10.1177/0734242X07079149.

Wolfe, K.L. and Shanklin, C.W. (2001) Environmental practices and management concerns of conference center administrators. *Journal of Hospitality & Tourism Research* 25(2), 209–216.

World Health Organisation (2020) Shortage of personal protective equipment endangering health workers. Available at: www.personal protective equipment endangering health workers worldwide (accessed August 2020).

World Travel and Tourism Council (WTTC) (2019) Economic impact research (2019). Available at: https://wttc.org (accessed July 2019)

9 Can Community-based Tourism be a Catalyst for Social Transformation?

Shivam Bhartiya[1]* and Vaibhav Bhatt[2]
[1]Department of Tourism and Hotel Management, Central University of Karnataka, Karnakata, India; [2]Deptartment of Tourism and Hospitality Management, Central University of Tamil Nadu, Tamil Nadu, India

Abstract

Opportunities generated by community-based tourism (CBT) support regional economic and social development leading to an increase in employment opportunities and the sustaining of local arts, culture and the environment. The research undertaken was exploratory and adopted qualitative techniques. The data for the study were collected with the help of interviews with the local people living in rural areas. The interview guidelines aimed to identify social and economic changes in terms of benefits and costs at both individual and community level, as perceived by the respondents. Furthermore, the study explored how tourism affected the life of the locals and that of the whole rural community. The thematic analysis of the interviews indicated that in the study area, tourism offered diverse job opportunities to locals and it also helped in the development of infrastructure and services for the community, which was observed as a positive effect of tourism. However, these positive effects were hampered by the increasing cost of goods and services, which were considered a consequence of tourism. According to some respondents, small tourism enterprises owned by the locals were not supported in the way that large companies were and they were neither involved by private companies nor by government institutions in the tourism decision-making process.

The results indicated that tourism development and associated population growth, with rapid urbanization of destinations, have led to several social and environmental problems because of the limited consideration given to local views on tourism planning and management. Identification of the costs and benefits of tourism planning and development is not only important for the economy of the destination but also its social transformation.

This study has revealed that CBT may be considered a factor of change, but the direction of this change is uncertain. This uncertainty presents challenges for tourism development initiatives that focus on local and regional growth. Thus, if development is intended to assist integral planning and the successful management of tourism enterprises, the perceptions of receiving communities must be considered in the tourism decision-making process.

Introduction

Rural communities everywhere in the world are facing the same issues of lack of infrastructure, out-migration and unemployment. Community-based tourism, nowadays, is considered one of the most important forms of tourism for integrated sustainable development of a tourism destination. It not only offers a variety of activities for tourists visiting the destination but it also provides employment opportunities and other socioeconomic development opportunities

*Corresponding author: shivam.prakash84@gmail.com

DOI: 10.1079/9781800621244.0009

at the destination. Many researchers (Russell, 2000; Yanes *et al.*, 2019; Stone and Stone, 2020) have credited CBT as an alternative form of tourism that involves local people in planning and maintaining tourism development. Russell (2000) highlighted that CBT should not only deliver social and economic benefits to the local population but it should also conserve and preserve local people's cultural identity and natural environment, along with their active support and involvement.

In the Himalayan region, various forms of tourism have emerged over the years such as CBT, ecotourism, homestay tourism, rural tourism, pilgrimage tourism and adventure tourism. There is a need for a tourism policy to make a clear distinction between the prevalent forms of tourism in the region and also to educate the local people, as the various forms of tourism are used synonymously in the region. Tourism development in the region is mostly monopolized by large organizations and the local community is neglected and ignored in the tourism decision-making process and is therefore unable to reap the social and economic benefits (Kala and Bagri, 2018).

This paper attempts to find whether CBT can lead to social transformation of the region, i.e. promotion and development of CBT in the Himalayan region will lead to integrated development of the region. The objective of the study is to identify the factors that help in the social transformation of the region through CBT.

Literature Review

The early 1990s saw the emergence of the social impacts of tourism (WCS, 1980; WTTC/UNCED, 1992; WTTC/WTO/ECC, 1995; UNWTO, 1996; UNEP/UNWTO, 2005;). A 'bottom-up' approach was initiated by researchers and practitioners of CBT during the era, which initiated participation of local people and focused on domestic tourism. By 2000, the distinction between CBT and commercial tourism markets was cemented; however, a number of fundamental challenges remained unresolved within CBT: integration within the broader community economy and development agendas; managing tourist desires for luxuries; and whether a community would

want or be able to develop tourism at all (Godde, 1998; TMI, 2000).

CBT is a tourism activity, community-owned and -operated, and managed or coordinated at community level, contributing to the wellbeing of the community through supporting sustainable livelihoods and protecting valued sociocultural traditions and natural and cultural heritage resources (ASEAN, 2016). This sustainable form of tourism started gaining acceptance as a way to mitigate the negative effects of mass tourism at the turn of the 21st century. The fundamental principle of CBT is community participation and organization by focusing on socially apt and responsible environmental development (Hiwasaki, 2006; Okazaki, 2008). Álvarez-García *et al.* (2018) stated that CBT is a form of sustainable tourism based on the community that aims to satisfy the needs of both residents and current tourists without compromising the needs of future generations who live at or visit the tourist destination. Thus, community tourism with a sustainable nature must aim at improving the living standards of residents while optimizing local economic benefits, minimizing the adverse effects of tourism, protecting the natural and built environment and providing a quality experience to visitors (Bramwell and Lane, 1993). Therefore, it is essential to promote the participation of the community in the tourism planning process where decision making involves all stakeholders and where the benefits have an impact on the community itself. The aim is to preserve the ethnic identity, values and cultural heritage of indigenous communities, while helping them to adapt to change and open their mentality, making them an essential part of the tourism product (López-Guzmán and Sánchez Cañizares, 2009).

As far as social transformation of the region through CBT was concerned, Mtapuri and Giampiccoli (2013) advocated that CBT should be entirely controlled by locals to mitigate the domination of external actors. The development of CBT should lead to the empowerment of locals by their participation in tourism-related activities, opening up new employment avenues and local development of infrastructure. Burgos and Mertens (2017) stated that with a growing interest in minimizing the harmful effects of tourism activities, which include communities being excluded from their benefits, CBT has emerged as a development model that connects tourism with community needs, centres local people within the planning process, and promotes equitable and sustainable practices. CBT is often considered to be a relevant strategy for community development as it promotes social inclusion, community empowerment, gender equity, and social and environmental sustainability.

Geographic Scope of the Study

The Garhwal Himalayas, situated between the latitudes of 29^0 26' to 31^0 28' N and longitudes 77^0 49' to 86^0 06' E, are blessed with a large number of river systems. The river Bhilangana is a major tributary of the Ganga in the Garhwal Himalayas. It originates from the Khatling glacier approximately 50 km south of the ice cave at Gaumukh at an elevation of 3717 masl. Earlier, the river Bhilangana flowed to a length of 95 km from its origin to join the river Bhagirathi at old Tehri. Bhilangana valley falls under the Tehri Garhwal district of Uttarakhand. The entrance to the valley is from Gadolia to Khatling glacier. The Bhilangana valley, draining the river of the same name, is a beautiful and relatively virgin valley. There is a well-trodden trekking route adjoining the Bhilangana valley. The region is well connected by road. Uttarakhand state transport buses ply the region throughout the year. The main town of Ghansali is well connected with the national capital (New Delhi) and the state capital (Dehradun) with the help of daily state transport buses and privately owned shared vehicles and taxis. The town of Ghansali is at a distance of 290 km and 110 km by road from New Delhi and Dehradun, respectively. The nearest railway stations are at Dehradun, Haridwar and Rishikesh. The stations are well connected with the rest of the country and one can easily book a train ticket to these stations from all major Indian cities. There are two domestic airports in the state of Uttarakhand, i.e. Jolly Grant airport in the Dehradun district and Pant Nagar in the Udham Singh Nagar district. The nearest airport to the study area is at Dehradun and, as mentioned earlier, one can

easily take a bus or a taxi from Dehradun to the town of Ghansali (Bhatt *et al.*, 2018).

Ghuttu, Ghansali, Akhori Tourism Circuit

The study area, i.e. Bhilangana valley in the Garhwal Himalaya, is endowed with nature's bounty with a basket of natural attractions that any tourist yearns for in a mountainous topography (Fig. 9.1). The valley has the majestic Khatling glacier, which is not only the source of the mighty Bhilangana river in the region but also attracts professional trekkers, mountaineers and researchers, both national and international, to the region. Important tourist attractions of the region include sites such as Akhori village, Reeh village, Gangi village, Ghuttu village, Khatling glacier, Sahastra Tal, Masar Tal, Kush Kalyan, Panwali Kantha and Matya Bugyal (Bhatt, 2018).

Methodology

The study was qualitative research carried out in the Ghuttu, Ghansali, Akhori tourism circuit of Bhilangana valley. Qualitative method was adopted as the researchers wanted to gain deeper insights from the people regarding the relationship between CBT and its role in social transformation of the region. Qualitative methods are helpful when utilizing numerous sources of evidence to investigate the contextual dimensions of complex issues in real-life circumstances and when the target group can be reached easily in their abode (Kala and Bagri, 2018). The researchers made several trips to the study area and had several rounds of discussions and meetings with the tourism stakeholders of the region, and, accordingly, a list of questions was prepared for the interview. Participants for the study were selected using purposive and snowball sampling methods. First, the researchers spoke with one person in the village and later he/she recommended the next person, and so on. An effort was made to include members of different age, gender, profession and income to capture diverse views regarding tourism development in the region. In total, 41 in-depth

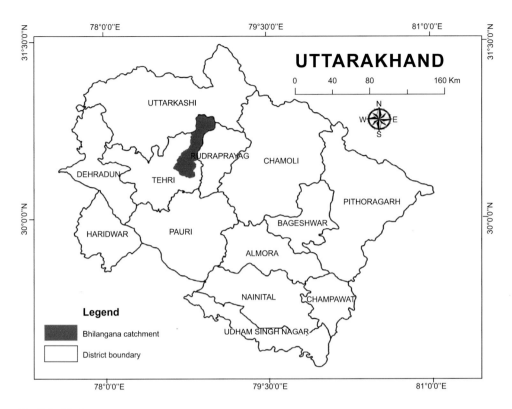

Fig. 9.1. Study area.
Source: Author's own map. Previously published in Bhatt and Bhartiya (2018)

interviews were completed. Themes and sub-themes were later analysed to draw inferences as per the objectives of the study (see Table 9.1).

Findings

The findings of the study revealed that the local community was deprived of the benefits of tourism development in the region due to the monopoly of big travel companies from Delhi and other cities nearby on organizing tours in the valley. One of the respondents, who owns a small teashop in Ghuttu village, stated that 'Ghuttu village has lot of tourism potential as it is the gateway for trekkers and nature lovers wanting to visit Khatling glacier and the other scenic meadows of the region, but the trekkers and nature lovers come in buses of Delhi-based travel companies and the local people of the region are only mute spectators unable to benefit

from the tourism potential of the region'. Based on the designed objectives and data collected with the help of in-depth interviews, researchers were able to identify the following factors in social transformation of the region:

1. **Availability of attractions in the region with immense tourism potential.** When the respondents were asked whether they agreed that the region has immense potential in terms of tourism, a majority of the respondents agreed with this statement. As said one respondent from Ghansali, 'The valley has some important tourism-specific locations such as Khatling glacier, Panwali Kantha, Kush Kalyan, Budha Kedar etc. ...which can attract lots of tourists to the valley interested in nature, adventure and pilgrimage tourism'. One resident of Akhori village informed the researchers that during the Kedarnath disaster of 2013, some of

Table 9.1. SWOT analysis of tourism in the study area.

Strengths	Weaknesses
• Presence of glaciers, mountains, meadows, waterfalls and snow-capped peaks • Perfect locations to savour the magnificence and beauty of the Himalayan ranges • Abundance of trekking trails • Presence of natural landscapes provides idyllic settings for nature tourism	• Absence of professionally trained and skilled tourist guides • Unplanned promotion in the region • Poor design quality in development of tourism facilities • Limited coordination among government agencies • Lack of efficient public transport • Poor involvement of the local community in tourism business • Inequitable distribution of tourism benefits among the local community
Opportunities	**Threats**
• Potential for nature tourism promotion at various places in the study area • Potential for wildlife tourism due to the abundance of floral and fauna • Opportunities for adventure tourism due to the availability of numerous trekking sites in the region • The cultural distinctiveness of the region can be utilized to attract rural and village tourists. • Opportunities for development of second homes/holiday homes in diverse sites of region	• Prone to natural disasters • Continued poor maintenance of roads and lack of effective visitor services discourage the arrival of quality tourist arrivals.

Source: Bhatt (2018).

the people took an alternative mountainous route to survive the floods and reached Akhori village. He suggested that an alternative route to reach Kedarnath temple should be explored from the Akhori village which will further increase the tourists' footfall in the valley.

2. **Unique Garhwali culture of the region.** The region has a unique Garhwali culture which cannot be experienced in any other part of the country. When the respondents were asked about the uniqueness of their culture, one elderly respondent from Akhori village stated that 'The food, music, dress attires and dance forms of the region are unique and can be experienced only by visiting the valley and interacting with the local community. But, over the years, due to the disinterest of people and their outmigration from the region to big cities such as Delhi and Dehradun in search of a better lifestyle, the culture of the region is slowly getting lost.'

When the respondents were informed by the researchers that their unique culture can be in demand with the promotion and development of CBT in the region, a majority of the respondents were of the opinion that they all would like to involve themselves in reviving the lost culture of the region through promotion and development of CBT.

3. **Improvement in quality of life of local people.** Researchers during their study trips to the valley found that the village population mostly comprised elderly people (mostly retired), schoolchildren and women. The villages had fewer adult males as they had moved out of their native places to big cities in search of employment. As one respondent of Ghuttu village said, 'Due to the lack of employment opportunities in the region, most of the people after their completion of education move to big cities in search of jobs and later settle there'. Another respondent stated that 'If development of tourism will

open up employment opportunities in the region, then the problem of outmigration will be solved as no one will move out of their villages and employment from tourism will improve their quality of lives'. The main source of income in the region was mostly agriculture and pastoralism. Tourism can be an alternative source of income for the local people.

4. **Improvement in infrastructure development.** The study area is a rural area with basic infrastructure and amenities available for the tourists as well as the local people. A primary survey indicated that the majority of the villages in the valley had a primary school, basic hospital facilities and road infrastructure. The villages of Ghuttu and Akhori had few lodging facilities and restaurants. Ghansali town had good availability of accommodation and food outlets. One of the respondents of Ghansali stated that 'Ghansali was the biggest town in the valley and the people from the nearby villages mostly come to Ghansali for their shopping needs'. A majority of the respondents were of the opinion that development of CBT in the region will improve the infrastructure of the region. An increase in tourism would increase the number of tourists and this will create the demand for better facilities and will eventually lead to improvement in the available infrastructure in the region, i.e. improved roads, better accommodation and food facilities, improvement in safety and security, 24-7 water and power supply, better medical facilities, etc.

5. **Source of income generation for local people.** Presently, the main source of income in the region is agriculture and pastoralism. Young people in the study area are interested in tourism jobs such as providing guide and trekking services to the tourists visiting the valley. One respondent in Ghuttu village stated that 'Mostly tourists come with big travel companies from Delhi and Dehradun and they do not interact much with the local people. Local people also do not have any training regarding trekking which can be useful for tourists. Local people are mostly involved in small jobs such as carrying the luggage of tourists or providing food to tourists.' The findings revealed

that the local people knew the potential of tourism in creating employment opportunities and increasing their income as they had seen such development in the villages in the Char Dham circuit. One respondent in Ghansali stated 'I do not know much about tourism...but I have seen the development in the areas en route [to] Kedarnath. If some of those tourists who visit Kedarnath also start visiting this region, then the entire area will be benefitted as tourism would develop the infrastructure and also provide new avenues to earn money.' The respondents were of the opinion that the government should take initiatives to promote the unique culture and tourism attractions of the valley so that tourists, after visiting the Char Dham, also visit this region.

6. **Creating environmental awareness.** The study area is rich in biodiversity with the presence of diverse varieties of flora and fauna. One of the hotel owners in Ghuttu stated that 'The meadows of Panwali Kantha during the rainy season are filled with colourful flowers and plant species which cannot be seen anywhere in the world. Also, people from outside who do not have much knowledge about the place set up camps at high altitudes and leave behind litter which harms the natural environment.' The respondents were of the opinion that the involvement of local people in tourism development and decision making would ensure that the effects of tourism do not harm the natural environment, and the money earned from tourism would be used for its preservation and conservation. Since the valley is their home, local people will never encourage tourism at the cost of harming the environment.

Conclusion

The study identified the various factors leading to social transformation of the region through CBT. The identified factors were: availability of attractions in the region with immense tourism potential; unique Garhwali culture of the region; improvement in quality of life of local people; improvement in infrastructure development; source of income generation for local people; and creating environmental awareness. Through the qualitative investigation, it was found that the local people of the region believed in all the above factors, which would eventually lead to social transformation of the region. The study revealed that tourism in the region is still in its early stages. Tourists visiting the valley are limited to extreme mountaineers, serious trekkers and researchers. Even though the region has lot of tourist attractions, a lot of work needs to be done in terms of promotion and communication and to create awareness among the tourists of the valley.

The tourists in the state of Uttarakhand are largely confined to visiting the Char Dham circuit, and not many tourists take a detour to visit the Bhilangana valley. Efforts need to be made by the government in the form of devising promotional strategies so that these hidden gems come into the mainstream tourism attractions of Uttarakhand. Government can also work towards setting up a tourism development agency in the region which would look after tourism development in the region and also take part in travel shows to promote the region.

Soft skills related to tourism should also be provided to the local community which will help them in understanding the nuances of tourism and also help them in interacting better with the tourists.

The study does not confirm that CBT will lead to social transformation of the region, as the study area is yet to see proper tourism development. From the local people's perspective, it was encouraging to know that the majority of them were positive and registered their agreement in developing CBT in the valley. The qualitative investigation revealed the attitude of the local community towards CBT by identifying factors for social transformation of the region. CBT can be a solution to a lot of problems of the region such as illiteracy, unemployment and outmigration. The development should be in a manner that equal opportunities are provided to all the members of the society. Tourism stakeholders should work together to ensure integrated tourism development in the region.

References

Álvarez-García, J., Durán-Sánchez, A. and del Río-Rama, M. (2018) Scientific coverage in community-based tourism: sustainable tourism and strategy for social development. *Sustainability* 10(4), 1158. DOI: 10.3390/su10041158.

ASEAN (2016) *ASEAN Community Based Tourism Standard*. ASEAN Secretariat, Jakarta.

Bhatt, V. (2018) *Nature Tourism Promotion in Bhilangana Valley of Garhwal Himalayas: Development Strategies and Prospective Planning*. Doctoral dissertation. HNB Garhwal University, India.

Bhatt, V., Bhartiya, S.P., Dhodi, R. and Dhodi, R.K. (2018) Impacts of nature tourism in a destination: a case study of Bhilangana Valley in Garhwal Himalaya. *South Asian Journal for Tourism and Heritage* 11(1), 33–45.

Bramwell, B. and Lane, B. (1993) Sustainable tourism: an evolving global approach. *Journal of Sustainable Tourism* 1(1), 1–5.

Burgos, A. and Mertens, F. (2017) Participatory management of community-based tourism: a network perspective. *Community Development* 48(4), 546–565. DOI: 10.1080/15575330.2017.1344996.

Godde, P. (1998) Community-based mountain tourism: practices for linking conservation with enterprise. In: *Synthesis of an Electronic Conference of the Mountain Forum*. April 13–May 18.

Hiwasaki, L. (2006) Community-based tourism: a pathway to sustainability for Japan's protected areas. *Society and Natural Resources* 19, 133–143. Available at: http://www.tandfonline.com/doi/abs/10.1080/08941920600801090 (accessed 29 December 2022).

Kala, D. and Bagri, S.C. (2018) Barriers to local community participation in tourism development: evidence from mountainous state Uttarakhand, India. *Tourism: An International Interdisciplinary Journal* 66(3), 318–333.

López-Guzmán, T. and Sánchez Cañizares, S.M. (2009) Turismo comunitario y generación de riqueza en países en vías de desarrollo. Un estudio de caso en el salvador. *REVESCO* 30, 85–103.

Mtapuri, O. and Giampiccoli, A. (2013) Interrogating the role of the state and nonstate actors in community-based tourism ventures: toward a model for spreading the benefits to the wider community. *South African Geographical Journal* 95(1), 1–15. DOI: 10.1080/03736245.2013.805078.

Okazaki, E. (2008) A community-based tourism model: its conception and use. *Journal of Sustainable Tourism* 16(5), 511–529. DOI: 10.1080/09669580802159594.

Russell, P. (2000) Community-based tourism. *Travel & Tourism Analyst* 5, 89–116.

Stone, M.T. and Stone, L.S. (2020) Challenges of community-based tourism in Botswana: a review of literature. *Transactions of the Royal Society of South Africa* 75(2), 181–193. DOI: 10.1080/0035919X.2020.1715510.

TMI (2000) *Community Based Tourism for Conservation and Development: A Resource Kit*. The Mountain Institute. Available at: www.mountain.org

UNEP/UNWTO (2005) *Making Tourism More Sustainable: A Guide for Policy Makers*. World Tourism Organisation, Madrid.

UNWTO (1996) *What Tourism Managers Need to Know: A Practical Guide to the Development and Use of Indicators of Sustainable Tourism*. World Tourism Organisation, Madrid.

WCS (1980) Secretariat/Focal Point. Cambridge: World Conservation Union (IUCN)/United Nation Economic Program (UNEP)/World Wildlife Fund (WWF).

WTTC/UNCED (1992) *Agenda 21: Adoption of Agreements on Environment & Development*. World Travel & Tourism Council Rio de Janeiro, Brazil.

WTTC/WTO/ECC (1995) *Towards Environmentally Sustainable Development*. World Tourism Organisation, Madrid.

Yanes, A., Zielinski, S., Diaz Cano, M. and Kim, S. (2019) Community-based tourism in developing countries: a framework for policy evaluation. *Sustainability* 11(9), 2506. DOI: 10.3390/su11092506.

10 Conclusion

Technological and social transformation are among the most important changes in a rapidly growing tourism and hospitality industry. Digital innovation is the engine of development and shows its impact on tourism and hospitality. The industry also brings positive changes to the social environment; it can support the community economically through employment, spending and infrastructure development; it brings investment to preserve local heritage, provide better livelihoods and local facilities, which in turn create better education, better leisure facilities, more frequent social events and a better lifestyle for the host community.

Over the years, tourism and hospitality has emerged as a major economic contributor and a source of social change. A steady increase in demand for travel ensures that the hospitality sector can forecast demand and unlock opportunities to make greater economic and social impact. Globally, sophisticated digital technologies have enabled new experiences – facial recognition, voice control, radio-frequency identification, chatbots, virtual reality (VR) experiences, and much more. The use of these new amenities has not only made travel more accessible but has also ensured safety and cleanliness, a must in the post-pandemic world.

In addition to technological developments, there is a plethora of social initiatives that have realized destinations' potential in tourism and hospitality and transformed the industry into a global source of integrated development.

However, there is another important element linked to the tourism and hospitality sector: adapting to new rules, standards and values, which have influenced and will continue to influence our society in terms of behaviour as consumers and service providers.

The rapid development of technology and social structure have brought immense changes in the industry. The era of digital tourism spaces supports a new generation of activities like VR or augmented reality (AR) spaces, and the instant analysis of customer reactions and behaviour supports the enhancement of their buying intentions. The traditional decision making processes are gradually being replaced with personalized offers, further increasing the importance of new digital technologies.

Greater emphasis is also put on social aspects, as host communities become as important as the tourists. Host communities express interest in novel forms of payment, which decreases the involvement of third parties. Thus, if social transformation is intended through tourism, hospitality and gastronomy, then perceptions of communities must be considered.

These technological and social transformations happen through a variety of processes, including: political upheaval and social movements; technological innovations and economic restructuring; response to environmental degradation and natural disasters; and changing values and cultural expressions.

These transformations are also a collective process, which require research-based expertise and resources rooted in equity, access and opportunity for all people, and democratic revitalization.

Overall, this transformation requires today's and tomorrow's leaders in tourism and hospitality to adapt. To prepare future tourism and hospitality stakeholders for the challenges of the digitally connected world and society, industry players need to adjust their working environment and culture.

© CAB International 2023. *Technology and Social Transformations in Hospitality, Tourism and Gastronomy: South Asia Perspectives* (eds S. Sharma and S. Bhartiya)
DOI: 10.1079/9781800621244.0010

Index

_____

CABI – who we are and what we do

This book is published by **CABI**, an international not-for-profit organisation that improves people's lives worldwide by providing information and applying scientific expertise to solve problems in agriculture and the environment.

CABI is also a global publisher producing key scientific publications, including world renowned databases, as well as compendia, books, ebooks and full text electronic resources. We publish content in a wide range of subject areas including: agriculture and crop science / animal and veterinary sciences / ecology and conservation / environmental science / horticulture and plant sciences / human health, food science and nutrition / international development / leisure and tourism.

The profits from CABI's publishing activities enable us to work with farming communities around the world, supporting them as they battle with poor soil, invasive species and pests and diseases, to improve their livelihoods and help provide food for an ever growing population.

CABI is an international intergovernmental organisation, and we gratefully acknowledge the core financial support from our member countries (and lead agencies) including:

ukaid
from the British people

Ministry of Agriculture
People's Republic of China

Australian Government
Australian Centre for
International Agricultural Research

Agriculture and
Agri-Food Canada

Ministry of Foreign Affairs of the
Netherlands

Schweizerische Eidgenossenschaft
Confédération suisse
Confederazione Svizzera
Confederaziun svizra

Swiss Agency for Development
and Cooperation SDC

Discover more

To read more about CABI's work, please visit: **www.cabi.org**

Browse our books at: **www.cabi.org/bookshop**,
or explore our online products at: **www.cabi.org/publishing-products**

Interested in writing for CABI? Find our author guidelines here:
www.cabi.org/publishing-products/information-for-authors/